Treating Nonepileptic Seizures

TREATMENTS THAT WORK

Editor-In-Chief

David H. Barlow, PhD

Scientific Advisory Board

Anne Marie Albano, PhD

Gillian Butler, PhD

David M. Clark, PhD

Edna B. Foa, PhD

Paul J. Frick, PhD

Jack M. Gorman, MD

Kirk Heilbrun, PhD

Robert J. McMahon, PhD

Peter E. Nathan, PhD

Christine Maguth Nezu, PhD

Matthew K. Nock, PhD

Paul Salkovskis, PhD

Bonnie Spring, PhD

Gail Steketee, PhD

John R. Weisz, PhD

G. Terence Wilson, PhD

✔ **TREATMENTS** THAT WORK

Treating Nonepileptic Seizures

THERAPIST GUIDE

W. CURT LAFRANCE, JR.
JEFFREY PETER WINCZE

OXFORD
UNIVERSITY PRESS

OXFORD
UNIVERSITY PRESS

Oxford University Press is a department of the University of
Oxford. It furthers the University's objective of excellence in research,
scholarship, and education by publishing worldwide.

Oxford   New York
Auckland   Cape Town   Dar es Salaam   Hong Kong   Karachi
Kuala Lumpur   Madrid   Melbourne   Mexico City   Nairobi
New Delhi   Shanghai   Taipei   Toronto

With offices in
Argentina   Austria   Brazil   Chile   Czech Republic   France   Greece
Guatemala   Hungary   Italy   Japan   Poland   Portugal   Singapore
South Korea   Switzerland   Thailand   Turkey   Ukraine   Vietnam

Oxford is a registered trademark of Oxford University Press
in the UK and certain other countries.

Published in the United States of America by
Oxford University Press
198 Madison Avenue, New York, NY 10016

© Oxford University Press 2015

Library of Congress Cataloging-in-Publication Data
LaFrance, Jr., W. Curt.
Treating nonepileptic seizures: therapist guide / W. Curt LaFrance, Jr., Jeffery Wincze.
pages cm. — (Treatments that work)
Includes bibliographical references.
ISBN 978–0–19–930717–3 (pbk. : alk. paper)
1. Convulsions—Treatment.   I. Wincze, Jeffery.   II. Title.
RC394.C77L34 2015
616.8′45—dc23
2014031732

About ✓ TREATMENTS THAT WORK

Stunning developments in healthcare have taken place over the last several years, but many of our widely accepted interventions and strategies in mental health and behavioral medicine have been brought into question by research evidence as not only lacking benefit, but perhaps inducing harm (Barlow, 2010). Other strategies have been proven effective using the best current standards of evidence, resulting in broad-based recommendations to make these practices more available to the public (McHugh & Barlow, 2010). Several recent developments are behind this revolution. First, we have arrived at a much deeper understanding of pathology, both psychological and physical, which has led to the development of new, more precisely targeted interventions. Second, our research methodologies have improved substantially, such that we have reduced threats to internal and external validity, making the outcomes more directly applicable to clinical situations. Third, governments around the world and healthcare systems and policymakers have decided that the quality of care should improve, that it should be evidence based, and that it is in the public's interest to ensure that this happens (Barlow, 2004; Institute of Medicine, 2001; McHugh & Barlow, 2010).

Of course, the major stumbling block for clinicians everywhere is the accessibility of newly developed evidence-based psychological interventions. Workshops and books can go only so far in acquainting responsible and conscientious practitioners with the latest behavioral healthcare practices and their applicability to individual patients. This new series, Treatments *ThatWork*, is devoted to communicating these exciting new interventions to clinicians on the front lines of practice.

The manuals and workbooks in this series contain step-by-step detailed procedures for assessing and treating specific problems and diagnoses. But this series also goes beyond the books and manuals by providing ancillary materials that will approximate the supervisory process in assisting practitioners in the implementation of these procedures in their practice.

In our emerging healthcare system, the growing consensus is that evidence-based practice offers the most responsible course of action for the mental health professional. All behavioral healthcare clinicians deeply desire to provide the best possible care for their patients. In this series, our aim is to close the dissemination and information gap and make that possible.

This *Therapist Guide* addresses the treatment of patients with nonepileptic seizures (NES), which frequently present in neurology, psychiatry, psychology, and emergency departments. The disorder has been documented in the medical literature for centuries, and much is known about the phenomenology, ictal semiology, neurologic signs, psychiatric comorbidities, neuropsychological testing, and psychosocial aspects of NES. Until recently, much less was known about the treatment of patients with psychogenic NES; however, new data on treatment are now available.

This *Therapist Guide* is the first treatment manual of its kind for clinicians, providing unique step-by-step strategies for treating patients with this debilitating disorder. It is designed to be used in conjunction with *Taking Control of Your Seizures: Workbook*, which patients should use during treatment. Used together, the *Therapist Guide* and *Workbook* facilitate communication between providers and patients with NES. Therapists who used the principles described in the *Therapist Guide* saw a significant decrease in seizure frequency, improvement in associated symptoms, and increased quality of life in their patients treated with the *Workbook*.

David H. Barlow, Editor-in-Chief,
Treatments *ThatWork*
Boston, Massachusetts

References

Barlow, D. H. Psychological treatments. *American Psychologist*, 2004; 59:869–878.

Barlow, D. H. Negative effects from psychological treatments: a perspective. *American Psychologist*, 2010;65(2): 13–20.

Institute of Medicine. *Crossing the Quality Chasm: A New Health System for the 21st Century*. Washington, DC: National Academy Press, 2001.

McHugh, R. K., & Barlow, D. H. Dissemination and implementation of evidence-based psychological interventions: a review of current efforts. *American Psychologist*, 2010;65(2): 73–84.

Contents

Acknowledgments

I am indebted to Joel Reiter and Donna Andrews for giving me permission to use their original *Epilepsy Workbook* in my research on patients with nonepileptic seizures (NES). In so doing, they have opened the door for patients with all types of seizures and related symptoms to "take control."

Thank you to the agencies who supported the clinical trials, including the American Epilepsy Society, Epilepsy Foundation of America, and National Institute of Neurological Disorders and Stroke. Many thanks to my many collaborators and research staff in the studies, who helped establish the evidence base for treating patients with NES with this intervention. Thank you to our patients and their families who participated in the studies and who provided helpful feedback on the *Workbook*. They have helped to improve the intervention and have taught us about caring for patients with seizures.

Thank you to the mentors who trained me in neurology, psychiatry, neuropsychiatry, neuropsychology, psychotherapy, and research. With a neuropsychiatric approach and perspective, providers are being equipped and patients with NES are being empowered to move out of the borderlands of neurology and psychiatry.

Thank you to the colleagues whom I have trained in this approach and who have made me critically examine the treatment with depth and rigor.

Thank you to my co-author Jeff Wincze in writing the *Therapist Guide* and to Joel Reiter for his help with editing. Thanks, also, to Heather Schatten for reviewing the manuscript to provide helpful clinical feedback.

Thanks to Craig Panner of Oxford University Press for connecting us with the OUP Treatments *ThatWork* team. We greatly appreciate the outstanding efforts of our editors—Sarah Harrington, Andrea Zekus, and Kate Scheinman—in making this work available for our colleagues to help patients with seizures embark on their journey to wellness.

WCL

Treating Nonepileptic Seizures

CHAPTER 1

Introductory Information for Therapists

Development of This Treatment Program and Its Evidence Base

Patients with psychogenic nonepileptic seizures (NES) frequently present in neurology, psychiatry, psychology, and emergency departments. The disorder has been documented in the medical literature for centuries, and much is known about the phenomenology, ictal semiology (i.e., seizure characteristics), neurologic signs, psychiatric comorbidities, neuropsychological testing, and psychosocial aspects of NES. For centuries, much less had been known about the treatment of patients with psychogenic NES; however, new data on treatment are now available from clinical trials, following the publication of the multidisciplinary-authored edition of *Gates and Rowan's Nonepileptic Seizures* (Schachter & LaFrance, 2010).

The aim of this *Therapist Guide* is to equip physicians, psychologists, therapists, nurses, and other clinicians with a validated treatment for psychogenic NES that will improve the lives of patients with this prevalent and disabling disorder.

This *Therapist Guide* is designed to facilitate communication between treating clinicians, consultants, patients with NES, and family members. It provides specific step-by-step guidelines for helping patients take control of their seizures and their lives. This "taking control" concept refers to the fact that many people with seizures, particularly those whose seizures are not fully controlled by medications, feel that their lives are "out of control." They may feel helpless, dependent, inadequate, and incapable of living a full and productive life. Treatment research studies using the *Workbook* and the authors' clinical experience in developing the treatment approach described in this *Therapist*

1

Guide have shown that positive results are possible when patients with seizures are offered a comprehensive program for improving seizure control and learning to take control of their lives.

The *Workbook* is a clinician-administered intervention in which the patient with psychogenic NES is assigned a chapter "Session" for each therapy appointment. The *Workbook* is designed to be used in conjunction with the *Therapist Guide*, and to facilitate communication between treatment provider and individual patients with NES. Included in the *Workbook* are step-by-step guidelines that will enable patients to take control of their seizures and their lives.

The author's clinical experience with NES and research in developing the treatment approach for NES directly informed the *Workbook* and treatment model. Patients treated with the intervention described in the *Therapist Guide* and *Workbook* have demonstrated improvements in seizures, comorbid symptoms, functioning, and quality of life. The author's work in training other clinicians to use the model directly informed the *Therapist Guide*.

The companion *Workbook* for this *Therapist Guide* was initially published as *Taking Control of Your Epilepsy: A Workbook for Patients and Professionals* by Joel Reiter, MD, Donna Andrews, PhD and Charlotte Janis, FNP. In 2002 Dr. LaFrance approached the Andrews / Reiter Epilepsy Research Program for permission to use the materials for patients with psychogenic nonepileptic seizures. Dr. LaFrance then tailored the original workbook to the issues specific to patients with NES and has treated patients with NES in clinical trials to assess its effectiveness. *Taking Control of Your Seizures: Workbook* is a collaborative project with the original authors.

Data from an open label trial for NES (LaFrance et al., 2009) and from a multi-site pilot randomized controlled trial (LaFrance et al., 2014), headed by the author, testing the treatment reveal a significant reduction in seizures *and* improvement in comorbid symptoms, including depression and anxiety, along with improved quality of life. The author personally provided the treatment while testing the *Workbook*, which is divided into 12 sessions (see Table of Contents for specific areas of focus), each with specific goals, obstacles, assignments, and tools. Patient acceptance of the intervention has been high, and feedback from patients and clinicians trained in the model has been used to modify the original epilepsy text to apply specifically to the needs of patients with NES.

This intervention will be appropriate for all clinicians who treat patients with psychogenic NES. Each patient is to purchase his or her own *Workbook* and use it to complete the weekly reading and assignments. The material is then reviewed in the scheduled therapy appointment with the clinician, who will use the *Therapist Guide* to discuss the weekly sessions.

The *Workbook* may also be of use to clinicians who treat patients with somatoform or other conversion disorders. The *Workbook* also has been used to treat patients with psychogenic movement disorders (PMD) with success (LaFrance & Friedman, 2009). Treatments of other chronic conditions are also being developed.

Training for seizure counselors is available through supervision. Interested professionals should contact Dr. LaFrance at Rhode Island Hospital, 593 Eddy Street, Providence, Rhode Island, USA, 02903. Phone 401-444-3534. Email: william_lafrance_jr@brown.edu.

Outline of This Treatment Program

Introduction for Clinicians

Training in this intervention involves becoming well versed in the content and experienced with the process. To be properly trained in the intervention is best accomplished by the following: Read through the entire *Workbook*. Know the material well. Your knowledge of the content will help you cover the material, while at the same time listening to the patient in session. The *Workbook* is used in conjunction with the *Therapist Guide*. After reading through the entire *Workbook*, re-read each *Workbook* session along with the corresponding *Therapist Guide* chapter to see the outline of each session and for examples of vignettes with clinicians and patients.

After mastering the content, becoming skilled in the delivery is the next step. For clinicians who desire proficiency in the delivery of this intervention, supervision in the intervention is necessary for expertise in treating patients with somatoform disorders. This is accomplished with weekly supervision sessions, in which video recordings of sessions using the *Workbook* are reviewed and discussed using two patients undergoing treatment. Successful completion of treating two patients with NES has proven to be a number that allows providers good exposure to common presentations and issues with this complex population as well as familiarity with the *Workbook* content and approach. Having supervision before beginning to use the intervention helps to: establish correct approaches with the treatment, become aware of similarities to and differences from other treatment approaches, and alert the clinician to the nuances and subtleties that are important for treating patients with somatoform disorders and that may differ from patients with mood or anxiety disorders. In supervision, the first patient helps the clinician gain familiarity with the content, and the second patient is for mastery of the intervention.

Structure of the Program

This program is designed to be delivered in 12 separate sessions, conducted individually. Each session will take approximately 50–60 minutes. (If more time is needed to review material or master content for specific sessions, another visit can be scheduled.) The treatment is designed with a schedule in which the therapist meets with the patients once weekly, where readings and various exercises will be assigned for the next meeting. Much of the work is done as the patient completes the *Workbook* session material and puts it into practice in their normal environment, during the week. (We have found that patients requesting a shorter course, trying to "squeeze in" a couple of sessions a week does not seem to give the patient enough time to process the content of the session.) Thus, preliminary evaluations yielding optimal results suggest that weekly sessions (i.e., one session a week) are the ideal manner for delivery of this program.

A typical timeline for the *Workbook* session appointments is as follows:

At initial encounter: Introduction for Patients (*Workbook* Chapter 1; *assigned to patient upon seizure monitoring unit discharge or at close of initial outpatient evaluation*)

Week 1: Making the Decision to Begin the Process of Taking Control (*Workbook* Chapter 2)

Who Will Benefit From This Program?

This *Therapist Guide* is designed to inform the treatment of people with psychogenic nonepileptic seizures (NES). The majority of patients with psychogenic NES will meet criteria for Conversion Disorder (300.11) according to the American Psychiatric Association's *Diagnostic and Statistical Manual of Mental Disorders* (1994), fourth edition (*DSM-IV*) and fifth edition (*DSM-5*). This maps to the ICD-10 diagnoses of Dissociative and Conversion Disorders (ICD-10 code, F44) or Dissociative convulsions (ICD-10 code, F44.5). Independent of the classification, patients with conversion disorder have a mixture of symptoms, discussed below.

What if Comorbid Problems Are Present?

In our experience, most patients with NES struggle with comorbid conditions, which often include depression, anxiety, and character pathology (personality disorders). Although there is no "ideal" or "pure" patient with NES with only one disorder and no other comorbidity for any condition, we have found that certain characteristics may portend a better outcome for the NES treatment. Acceptance of the NES diagnosis is important for optimal benefit in this program. Patients who embrace the diagnosis and are "on board" with the treatment fare better than those who insist that they are having epileptic seizures despite video EEG evidence to the contrary, or who believe that the doctors are missing a diagnosis. Before treatment can proceed, the clinician may help resistant patients with NES understand that their seizures reflect an underlying psychological issue. Patient motivation is also a critical variable. Motivation is demonstrated via appointment attendance and successful completion of therapy homework prior to sessions. Patients with good insight and at least a moderate reading ability appear to respond better to the treatment than less insightful patients or patients who struggle with basic reading difficulties. Personality disorders are common in NES, and those with engrained characterological issues may take longer to derive improvement than those who do not. Age does not appear to be a predictor of response.

Potential obstacles include severe self-destructive character pathology, financial secondary gain, limited cognitive ability, current substance abuse or dependence, psychosis, and the level of the patient's distress. These obstacles, however, do not preclude treatment, and some patients with these disorders have made changes and choices that promote controlling their seizures.

Assessment

The diagnosis of NES is made with a comprehensive neurologic and psychiatric history, neurologic and psychiatric examination, and is confirmed with video EEG, which is the gold standard for diagnosis (LaFrance et al., 2013). The history and exam will identify predisposing, precipitating, and perpetuating factors (LaFrance et al., 2002). Using video EEG, the ictus (seizure, event) is captured on video and is observed simultaneously with the EEG tracing. Epileptic seizures reveal the typical epileptiform wave forms, and NES reveal no epileptiform activity. While a small amount of epileptic seizures can have "scalp negative" EEG, these can be diagnosed by their stereo-typed semiology. If a patient has different types of seizures (e.g. "the staring ones, usually after I have an argument, and the ones at night where I wake up on the floor with bruises and I've bitten the side of my tongue and wet myself"), both semiologies should be captured on video EEG to differentiate the NES from the epileptic seizures. If video EEG is not available, encourage the patient and family to video the event with their own equipment and show it to the neurologist/epi-leptologist. Observing the semiology of the seizure is extremely helpful for aiding the diagnosis of NES. The therapist should have a copy of the video EEG report prior to treatment.

Medication

Many patients with NES have already met with healthcare providers prior to receiving the NES diagnosis. Given the diagnostic complexity of this population, which frequently includes comorbid diagnoses, the majority of these patients are already taking medication by the time they present to a mental health professional. Common medications include anticonvulsant/antiepileptic drugs (AEDs), selective serotonin reuptake inhibitors (SSRIs), mixed mechanism antidepressants, tri-cyclic antidepressants, monoamine oxidase inhibitors (MAOIs), and benzodiazepines. There is no medication that has been proven to stop NES completely. Chapter 3 of the *Workbook* focuses on common central nervous system (CNS) medications and their mechanisms of action. The chapter is designed to empower patients to take control of their medication regimen. While it is not the goal of this treatment to taper patients off all of their medications, patients might make differ-ent decisions about their medications after learning more about them. While AEDs treat epilepsy, they do not treat NES. In fact, research has demonstrated that AEDs may actually increase nonepileptic sei-zures. AEDs may be taken for indications other than epilepsy, such as migraine prophylaxis, bipolar mood disorder, or certain pain condi-tions. So, some patients with NES may continue AEDs, but not to treat their NES. Thus, patients with lone NES who read the chapter and discuss medications with their therapist might opt out of taking AEDs if they do not have a diagnostic indication for those medications.

Who Should Administer the Program?

This program is designed to be administered by clinicians who are familiar with somatoform disorders, which can include psychiatrists, psychologists, therapists, counselors, neurologists, nurses, and social workers.

Although the *Workbook* is designed as a bibliotherapy resource, the *Workbook* is not designed to be a "self-help" book; it is strongly recommended that patients work with a provider or mental health professional who is well versed in this treatment. While traditional cognitive behavioral therapy (CBT) treatments may be assignment-based and may be attempted by some patients without supervision, the *Workbook* approach and assignments are multifaceted, CBT-informed psychotherapy (CBT-ip), incorporating different therapeutic modalities. Attempting to use the *Workbook* without the guidance of a trained professional might prove to be overwhelming to the patient due to the complex nature of the NES diagnosis and issues explored.

Full Workbook Versus Installments

As outlined in the timeline above, *Workbook* chapters should be assigned in installments for appointments, rather than as completing the full book. In our experience with bibliotherapy, we have found that having patients read the entire *Workbook* all at once could undermine the treatment process. To pace the therapy, the therapist can assign the *Workbook* sessions prescribing the next week's chapter "dose" at the end of each appointment. At each visit, the patient brings the completed *Workbook*, his or her journal, and any other loose paperwork in a binder, organized for each appointment. Over time, with a full armentarium, all of the work done remains with the patient, kept for his or her future reference when relevant issues may arise again.

To illustrate the point, traditional CBT for most psychiatric problems involves a combination of readings and exercises designed to address specific aspects of a disorder. For example, treatment for panic disorder with agoraphobia involves psychoeducation, readings, interoceptive exposures, cognitive restructuring, and in vivo exposures. Providing the entire treatment manual all at once might prove to be too overwhelming for patients who "read ahead" about upcoming therapy sessions. If a patient with panic attacks reads ahead and learns about upcoming situational exposures, for example, the patient might opt to drop out of treatment due to a belief that she or he could never engage in such exposures. However, if this same patient worked with a therapist utilizing the installment method, the patient will feel prepared to do situational exposures. Other patients who read upcoming sections might insist that what they read about "won't work for me." By assigning the treatment in sections, the therapist has the ability to incrementally manage what information is being disseminated. This measured approach builds confidence in the applicability for many skeptical patients over time.

Every patient is unique, and although the treatment *Workbook* is designed to treat anyone with psychogenic NES or other conversion diagnosis, we acknowledge that "one size does not fit all." Specifically, a therapist might determine that certain sections are unnecessary for their particular patient and may be considering withholding a section from the patient's treatment. For example, a therapist may think a treatment section that involves family members might be withheld from a patient who does not have family members who can participate in session assignments. We, however, would not recommend skipping or "withholding" sessions. Content in each session is derived from seeing hundreds of patients with seizures, and it targets known areas of pathology in the population with seizures. We, therefore, recommend, give the patient "the full dose" working through all the sessions of the *Workbook*, with the patient.

Timing is important. The introductory session might prove to be invaluable for patients diagnosed with NES in the seizure monitoring unit (SMU) and can serve as a segue to treatment initiation with NES counselors. The *Workbook* can be provided by the unit or provider and the introductory section can be assigned by the epileptologist, neurologist, or consulting mental health provider as a tangible task in preparation for the first outpatient appointment with the seizure counselor. If a psychiatrist or psychologist is part of the SMU team, he or she can introduce the *Workbook* as a key component to care for the patient with NES and emphasize the importance of outpatient follow-up.

Homework Assignments

Awareness is one step toward change, but it must be paired with *action*. One of the mainstays of traditional CBT that distinguishes it from other therapies is the frequent assignment of homework. CBT involves numerous tools, skills, and techniques that patients must practice outside of therapy sessions in order to assimilate session material. Homework is designed to dovetail with session material and should be clearly explained prior to the conclusion of each session and thoroughly reviewed at the beginning of the next session. Successful completion and practice of therapy homework enables patients to "become their own therapist," as they gain skills and continue to self-manage, once treatment ends. In the *Workbook*, homework for each session is found at the conclusion of each chapter. The "moment of truth" comes when the patient comes to the appointment and he or she reviews the material with the therapist. During the appointment, the patient's workbook is placed where both patient and therapist can see it and is used to review the session material. The patient can turn to the pages to read the written responses he or she wrote or to discuss the sentences or concepts he or she identified that were important to them. The *Workbook* is a very hands-on tool used during the appointment.

How the *Workbook* Gets Completed

Each *Workbook* chapter needs to be fully completed by the patient in the time *prior to* each appointment. How that is done may differ from patient to patient. The optimal approach is for the patient to write out responses to each task or question in the actual *Workbook*. Some patients, however, keep their notes on a computer. Some may bring in a spreadsheet in the format of the assignment. While some may prefer this approach, writing the responses in the *Workbook* itself will promote organization and easy retrieval of the material when they refer back to it. In our experience, when patients complete assignments using other notebooks, sheets of paper, etc., they sometimes forget to bring these supplementary materials to their appointments. Encouraging them to complete all assignments in the *Workbook* and keeping them in a binder is a way to better ensure that completed work is brought to their appointments.

As noted above, this CBT-informed psychotherapy treatment also has elements of other psychotherapeutic approaches, including interpersonal, psychoeducational, motivational interviewing, self-efficacy/self-management, dialectical, and psychodynamic modalities. Given the wealth of information provided to patients in this *Workbook* treatment program, it might be tempting to adopt a "lecturing" style in session. However, research has shown that patients assimilate information better if they make connections on their own. Therapists are strongly encouraged to adopt a Socratic teaching style. For example, when reviewing the content of a previous session, ask the patient what his or her understanding of the ideas presented is, rather than telling the patient what he or she "learned." In other words, resist the common clinician educator's temptation to be pedantic.

One major difference between how this intervention differs from manual-based therapies for psychiatric disorders, such as panic disorder, is how it is administered. A major tenet of this treatment for NES is the patient establishing an internal locus of control. In traditional cognitive-behavioral manual-based therapies, the therapist takes on the role of "teacher." Each therapy session becomes an opportunity for the therapist to present new material and then send the patient home with readings and other exercises that dovetail with what was taught on that day. The readings and exercises are used to solidify session ideas.

What differentiates this seizure treatment manual from other bibliotherapy treatments is that each session is given to the patient *ahead of time to complete* and discuss the completed work in their next appointment. Rather than "teaching" the material, the material is processed in the appointment *after* the patient has reviewed it and has completed readings and exercises. This approach makes *the patient* responsible for learning the material, thus establishing an internal locus of control.

Another differentiating point for this approach compared to other modalities involves the psychotherapeutic technique of interpretation, that is, keeping that in check. The role of the therapist in this intervention is to hold up a mirror where the patient can look at himself without the façade he wears for the world (or for himself). The mirror is a non-judgmental, non-condemning reflection of who the patient is. The therapist who interjects interpretations too often and too easily can shift into the role of an artist (inappropriately). Again, the therapist is not creating a painting, rather, he is holding a reflecting glass. The patient may choose to take the narrative that is being constructed from a life of chaos, modifying past scars to create a new present and future for himself. In this process, the therapist can try too hard sometimes with working to "ask just the right question" or wax interpretively to get the patient to a place that the therapist has targeted as important. With good therapy, the patient will come to that place, in time. During this process, the therapist can remind herself that she should not be the artist but rather the easel who holds the mirror for the patient.

Patients Who Invest Time and Effort in the *Workbook* Will Refer to the *Workbook* After Treatment Ends

Through working with a trained seizure counselor, the *Workbook* can help patients effectively take control of their seizures. For the seizures that may continue after treatment ends, the *Workbook* is a valuable resource for the patient if, over time, portions of the treatment are forgotten. The *Workbook* can also be used for post-treatment, future review sessions with the counselor if the patient believes that a "booster" session is necessary after completing the material. Future sessions may involve family members if family dysfunction is identified as a perpetuating factor to persistent seizures. The patient should be encouraged to periodically review materials found in the *Workbook* as a way to "cement" the treatment information.

Issues Encountered

Which Patients Should Receive the Intervention?

Selecting a patient who is not interested in pursuing therapy can be gauged in comparison with the decision to prescribe the right medication for the right patient at the right time. Not every patient is willing to take a medicine or pursue a treatment, even if it may help. To illustrate, smokers or drinkers who do not want to quit, won't—even with the best pills and programs available for abuse/dependence disorders. Similarly, prescribing an antibiotic to someone who has an infection but is not willing to ingest/apply it for the necessary treatment course (or at all) is of no use. Moreover, prescribing to someone who does not believe he has an infection can yield low compliance.

The right medication for the right disorder also is important. To illustrate, prescribing an antibiotic for a viral infection will have no impact on the underlying viral infection, or as another example, an antibiotic that is not sensitive to the causative bacterium will not clear the infection. While this treatment *Workbook* can be administered to anyone with seizures, it may not be for all patients with seizures, depending on whether they are willing and ready to engage in therapy. The idea of gauging clinical appropriateness of prescribing is not "cherry-picking"; rather, it is applying the right treatment to the right patient, for the right indication, at the right time. As is the case in addictions interventions, ultimately, you cannot force a treatment on someone who does not think she needs it.

Which Patients Could Receive the Intervention?

Patients with seizures, including epileptic seizures or psychogenic NES, and who may also have other conversion symptoms, including psychogenic movement disorder, astasia-abasia, weakness, sensory symptoms, cognitive complaints, and other psychiatric comorbidities, including depression, anxiety, personality disorders, and/or pain, have demonstrated benefit from the intervention. Patients sometimes come to appointments noting, "The things I am learning for the seizures are also helping with my other symptoms." Ultimately, the principles prescribed in the *Workbook* to apply to seizures can generalize to comorbidities and may result in improvement in those areas, also.

What About Disability?

Many patients with chronic, recurrent, seizures are not able to drive. That may influence their ability to get to work. Some may work with heavy equipment. Patients will sometimes bring disability paperwork for a clinician to sign or will request an out of work letter to their employer. Different clinicians take different stances on a response to this request. Our practice has been to notify the patient that there are two roles for health care providers, one of the treating clinician and one who addresses functioning (e.g. disability evaluation). The treating clinician can focus on treatment with an ultimate goal of helping the patient return to functioning. With the patient's permission, the treating clinician can release the records to the case reviewer. Separately, an independent evaluator can review treatment notes and progress to aid in determining disability status. Separating these roles may limit potential for bias. Regarding preparedness, having a seizure protocol paper available for work for employers or school for nurses or teachers can help in those settings if seizures occur at work or school.

> ✓ **Clinician Note**
>
> *Realize that comorbidities are the* rule *and not the exception, so patients with comorbid diagnoses are not excluded from treatment. Heterogeneity* is *their homogeneity.* The seizure counselor should conduct a comprehensive assessment prior to fully engaging in the treatment, identifying psychiatric comorbidities, personality disorders/traits, neurologic and medical history and lab / EEG / imaging workup and social / developmental history, including trauma and abuse.

In What Setting Should the *Workbook* Material be Delivered?

The studies for NES using the *Workbook* were conducted administering the sessions in outpatient individual therapy appointments. Acknowledging that, many have asked if this material can be administered in the outpatient group therapy setting. While a formal group trial using the *Workbook* has not been completed, open label pilot trials using other group therapy approaches for patients with NES have shown preliminary evidence of improvement in symptoms or in understanding of the disorder. With that in mind, one option for a group therapy approach is to have each patient obtain their own *Workbook* and bring the completed session to a group appointment for discussion with a therapy leader. Discussions are underway to apply the *Workbook* in a formal group therapy trial.

Setting Appropriate Expectations for the Therapist

Some therapists may have reservations about manualized therapies. Concerns may have included loss of therapist autonomy, feeling constrained in addressing relevant areas while working with another topic, not addressing the complexity of the seizure population, or not having time to cover the session material. In actuality, the *Workbook* provides structure to navigate the complexity of the patient's life with NES. This therapy is a *patient-led, therapist-guided* approach. The *Workbook* targets known areas of pathology and interpersonal challenges in the population, providing a psychosocial map to course through these difficult areas. If a patient brings up an issue of importance in the appointment, the therapist pays attention and listens to the patient. The comment or issue may have been prompted by the patient's review of the session material. The comment can be woven into session content discussion during the appointment. Ultimately, the *Workbook* is *not* a rigid text to be "taught" and reviewed in the appointment, rather, the *Workbook* is a handmaiden to the therapist to give support and structure when discussing important and challenging issues.

Setting Appropriate Expectations for the Patient

The work will be done by the patient, and the therapist will walk with the patient through the material over time. This is the therapeutic process of "abiding" (or bearing with the patient). As the therapist establishes hope and bears with the patient, the patient can enter a place of knowing him- or herself and of personal transformation. See Chapter 16, "When a Patient Has a Seizure in the Office Setting," for more on the essential concept of abiding. This therapeutic process may not be an immediate fix, but with awareness (insight) and action (work), many patients describe experiencing a transformation with this work and have taken control of their seizures and other symptoms as they develop a new sense of agency.

CHAPTER 2

Introductory Session: Understanding Seizures

(Corresponds to *Workbook* Chapter 1)

MATERIALS NEEDED/TASKS

- Seizure Log (one for prior week and one blank for future week)
- Patient's completed Session Intro, "Introduction for the Patient: Understanding Seizures"
- Session 1: "Making the Decision to Begin the Process of Taking Control," to assign at end of appointment

APPOINTMENT OUTLINE

When reviewing the Introductory Session

- Review Seizure Log.
- Review the different types of seizures.
- Ask the patient to discuss her thoughts on her own seizure type(s).
- Begin discussion of the patient's understanding of psychogenic NES and conversion disorder.
- Review any past history, diagnoses, workup, EEGs documenting NES.
- Review the figure: Five Aspects of Your Life Experiences, and the relationship of the areas to each other.
- Review the patient's answers to the Worksheet: Situations, Moods, Thoughts.
- Assign homework: Session 1.
- Confirm next appointment time and date.

One of the first "lessons" communicated to patients with NES is distinguishing epilepsy from NES. The Introductory Session describes similarities and differences between epileptic and nonepileptic seizures. For the clinicians who are or will be treating patients with NES, here is a brief overview of NES and its roots in conversion disorder.

A Brief History of Conversion Disorder and Nonepileptic Seizures

A conversion disorder diagnosis was made historically when a thorough neurological or medical workup had ruled out etiologies for the constellation of somatic symptoms that a patient experiences. Traditionally the word "conversion" reflected the hypothesis that a patient's symptoms were being "converted" from unresolved unconscious processes into a physical presentation.

Early Egyptian and Greek medical texts from 2,000 years ago describe "hysteria," which reflected a belief that a woman's unusual symptom presentation (e.g., globus hystericus, paralysis, or convulsions) was caused by her "wandering womb," which had detached and was floating around her body out of frustration of disuse. Fortunately, we have made great progress in understanding patients with conversion disorder.

Although the link between epilepsy and hysteria continued to evolve throughout the eighteenth and nineteenth centuries with work by Charcot and Gowers, the Viennese neurologist Sigmund Freud (1856–1939) popularized the notion of conversion when he suggested that there was a connection between past trauma and the psychological conversion of that trauma into somatic symptoms.

During the twentieth century, the link between stress, conversion and nonepileptic seizures was especially evident in returning World War I combat Veterans who were diagnosed with "shell shock." Many of these soldiers did not experience any physical harm to their bodies, but they exhibited the same physical symptoms as had been noted in civilians from earlier medical texts, and the syndrome continues to persist in civilians and in Veterans, today. Similar cases were and are also seen

[Handwritten margin notes: "Seizure = Body's of way of expressing distress"]

during World War II, the Korean War, Vietnam War, Gulf War and Operation Iraqi Freedom/Operation Enduring Freedom.

Today, there is growing acceptance that NES is the body's way of expressing psychological distress. Conversion symptoms are a disorder of communication, where the patient expresses distress in somatic symptoms rather than in a healthy verbal manner. The advent of video EEG monitoring in the 1960s has been paramount in distinguishing between epileptic and nonepileptic seizures. Today, video EEG is used to confirm the diagnosis of NES, as described below.

Making the Diagnosis of NES

As noted in the introduction to this *Therapist Guide*, the gold standard for NES diagnosis uses video EEG. A diagnosis of documented NES is made with video EEG showing no epileptiform activity before, during, or after the ictus, and semiology consistent with NES, along with a history and exam presentation consistent with conversion disorder. Some clinicians use the terminology "dissociative seizures" for the events, but whether they are referenced as "dissociative," "conversion," or "psychogenic" is less important for treatment than getting to the root of the symptoms with the patient. The *DSM-5* criteria for conversion disorder (a.k.a. functional neurological disorder) include the following:

- One or more symptoms are present that either affect voluntary motor or sensory function or cause transient loss of consciousness.
- The symptom or deficit is, after medical assessment, not better explained by another medical condition, or mental disorder.
- Clinical findings provide evidence of incompatibility between the symptoms and recognized neurological or medical conditions.
- The symptom or deficit causes clinically significant distress or impairment in social, occupational, or other important areas of functioning or warrants medical evaluation.
- *Note*: A relevant psychological stressor is often present but is not a requirement to establish the diagnosis. (Patients do not always feel comfortable sharing trauma in a brief, initial encounter.)
- *Note*: Proving the absence of feigning is not a requirement to establish the diagnosis. (Malingered or feigned symptoms are not considered functional.)

These criteria changed with the publication of *DSM-5* to include incorporating non-neuroanatomic semiology as one of the criteria and moving the psychological stressor and absence of feigning to a note.

Fear-Avoidance Model of Nonepileptic Seizures

The fear-avoidance model for psychogenic NES posits that the patient has been exposed to a threatening situation or traumatic event(s) that has not been properly processed. While not all patients have a history of trauma, the majority of patients with NES do. Other patients may have had a developmental history with emotional privation. These precursors may be the background to a patient with NES developing a belief that the past or present is too overwhelming to confront, or a feeling of being ill-equipped to address internal or external conflict. As a result of suppressing this negative event or history, the patient experiences fear and anxiety, which is unconsciously expressed via NES. Thus, NES constitutes a maladaptive way to cope with a past trauma and/or current stressors, leading to unremitting stress. Catastrophic thinking feeds NES episodes and avoidance of things that one fears promote more NES, which eventually leads to disability, depression, and convalescence, which feeds future NES. This is a vicious cycle, which then repeats itself (see Figure 2.1). The treatment involves allowing the patient to make the connections in this vicious cycle, and then equipping him or her to break the connections. When a patient no longer fears having NES, which occurs via confronting the fears and situations, rather than avoiding them, recovery is possible.

Defining Seizures

This *Therapist Guide* is intended to guide treatment providers through the process of helping patients take control of their seizures.[1] The approach outlined in the patient *Workbook* is unique in that it emphasizes a partnership between the patient, physician, and seizure counselor in which all work together toward the effective management of the patient's seizure disorder.

---

[1] The following material summarizes *Workbook* Chapter 1, "Introduction for the Patient: Understanding Seizures."

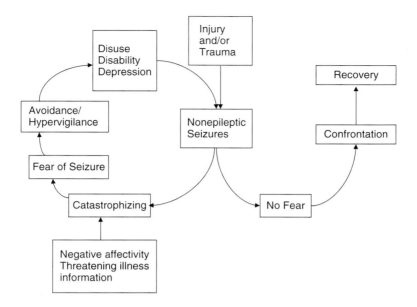

Figure 2.1

The Fear Avoidance Model for Psychogenic Nonepileptic Seizures (NES).

Reprinted from LaFrance & Bjoranes, from Schachter, S.C., & LaFrance, W.C., Jr., eds., *Gates and Rowan's Nonepileptic Seizures*, 3rd ed. Cambridge; New York: Cambridge University Press, 2010, p. 271, with permission of Cambridge University Press.

What Is a Seizure?

Most patients with NES lack basic knowledge about seizures. For many, the word "seizure" connotes something frightening and dangerous. This introductory section serves to provide psychoeducation about epileptic seizures and nonepileptic seizures.

Seizures are common and are characterized by recurring time-limited episodes of changes in behavior, movement, senses, with or without an alteration of consciousness, during which the person may or may not be aware of his or her surroundings. Seizures typically last from a few seconds to several minutes. In some people, seizures may also involve involuntary movements of the arms, legs, or face, strange feelings, or sensations, and sometimes bowel or bladder incontinence. Sometimes seizures have a known cause, such as a head injury, infection of the brain, or tumor. Epileptic seizures are caused by abnormal brain cell function, and are associated with epileptic activity on an electroencephalogram (EEG). Other seizures occur that are not associated with abnormal brain cell function, and when observed on video EEG, these events are not associated with epileptic EEG activity. These events are referred to as nonepileptic seizures (NES). NES may be caused by stress, anxious or depressed emotions, past traumatic or neglect experiences.

Why Is It Important for Patients to Understand Their Seizure Disorder?

It is important for patients to understand as much as possible about their seizures for two main reasons. The first reason is that often the fear of having a seizure does more damage than the seizures themselves. An individual with seizures may consider him- or herself an invalid who has a frightening, unpredictable disease, unless he or she learns about the condition, including the fact that the vast majority of people with seizures are able to lead full and active lives.

The second reason for making the effort to understand seizures is that this understanding is often the key to reducing the frequency of seizures and the ill effects that seizures may have on the patient's life as a whole. Even if seizures are eliminated by medications, knowing about one's condition can help patients to cope positively and to maintain good seizure control throughout his or her life.

The more patients learn about the multitude of factors in their lives that affect their health in general, and their seizures in particular, the more patients will be able to contribute to the effectiveness of this treatment program.

Diagnosing Seizures

The onset of seizures can be a dramatic and frightening event. As such, it is important to clarify the process of diagnosing seizures in order to identify the kind of seizure(s) the patient is experiencing, as well as the likely cause of those seizures. Explain to the patient that her physician will take a detailed history and will perform a series of medical tests, including an EEG or a video EEG, if she has not already had the test(s).

After this complete medical investigation, usually the patient's physician will be able to tell if the seizures were caused by known damage to the brain (such as accident or illness). If the term "idiopathic" or "unknown cause" was used in a prior explanation, explain that it means that medical science does not understand the physiologic reason for the seizures and that her body and brain appear otherwise healthy.

What Are the Different Kinds of Seizures?

Seizures are divided among three categories:

- epileptic
- physiologic nonepileptic events (PNEE)
- psychogenic nonepileptic seizures (NES)

The simple distinctions are as follows:

- Epilepsy is caused by abnormal brain cell firing.
- PNEE is caused by a metabolic or medical issue, but it is not epilepsy.
- Psychogenic NES are caused by underlying psychological conflicts or stressors, and are many times associated with depression, anxiety, trauma, or personality issues. NES are not epilepsy.

There are several kinds of seizure presentations (or semiologies) that may occur in any of the three seizure types. The most common ways seizures appear are described in now dated terminology, including the following:

1. **Generalized tonic clonic or "Grand mal" seizures:** With no warning or minimal warning, such as dizziness or a full feeling in the stomach, a person loses consciousness, stiffens, and jerks about.
2. **Absence or "Petit mal" seizures:** For a few seconds, the person loses contact and "spaces out." Onset for this type of seizure is usually prior to age 20.
3. **Complex partial seizures (focal dyscognitive seizures):** A person loses contact with his or her surroundings, and cannot communicate. Often there are movements such as smacking of the lips, wringing of the hands, jerking or tightening of an arm or leg. These seizures may be preceded by a warning known as a "pre-seizure aura."

4. **Myoclonic seizures**: Quick, lightning-like jerks of the limbs, head, or body, usually not associated with change in level of consciousness.

5. **"Drop attacks" or Atonic seizures**: A person loses awareness and quickly drops to the ground. Injuries may occur with the falls.

Psychogenic nonepileptic seizures can resemble any of the semiologies described above; however, when the events are observed on video EEG, no epileptic activity is observed. These seizures are many times associated with depression, anxiety, trauma, or personality traits.

What Is the Physician's Role in Treating Seizures?

A physician—usually a neurologist or epileptologist—can assist by diagnosing the type of seizures your patient has and determining the probable cause of these seizures. Epileptic seizures are best treated by neurologists. Nonepileptic seizures are best treated by mental health professionals, including psychiatrists, psychologists, or counselors, who are familiar with NES treatments. The patient's physician might also select and prescribe medications, as well as ordering periodic lab tests to help determine the amount of medicine needed to reduce the frequency of the patient's epileptic seizures, if a patient has both epileptic and nonepileptic seizures (which occurs in approximately 10% of patients). Another important role of the physician is to clearly explain the beneficial reasons for taking medications, as well as the possible side effects, or to recommend stopping certain medications.

In addition, the approach outlined in this *Therapist Guide* suggests a new role for the clinician: that of assisting the patient to "take control" of all aspects of his life, including seizures and the effect that seizures have on his health and well-being. Most patients with NES will be referred for therapy by a physician.

What Is the Patient's Role?

The standard medical approach to seizures assigns the patient a narrow role—that of taking medicines regularly as prescribed. While this is an important responsibility, research shows that there are many additional factors besides drug therapy that determine whether seizure frequency is reduced and whether the patient learns to cope effectively with having seizures. For example, learning to recognize prodromal symptoms prior to a seizure and identifying the major life stresses that affect seizure frequency are important steps in gaining control and learning to cope successfully.

It is important to emphasize that no counselor, family member, or friend can do this work of self-observation and self-discovery for the patient. Only active participation in this process will enable the patient to reach his or her optimal level of wellness, including seizure control. The patient is the most important person in this process of taking control of his or her seizures. The goal of this time-limited therapy process is to allow patients to develop agency, as they gain increasingly greater responsibility for their health, their seizures, and for finding life fulfillment.

What Is Your Role as Seizure Counselor?

For many patients referred to a seizure counselor, this will be their first meeting with a psychiatrist or a neurologist (MD), a psychologist (PhD), a licensed counselor such as a marriage family therapist (MFT), or a licensed social worker (LSW) a nurse (RN), a nurse practitioner (NP), a health educator, or a lay person who has had personal experience with seizures. Meeting with a seizure counselor for the first time might be a daunting experience for the patient. Because you will be working with your patients for a period of time on aspects of their personal lives, it is important to establish rapport during your first meeting with the patient. Make sure you have taken and know the patient's history. Ultimately, the experience that patients gain from working with a seizure counselor can be shared with others, such as family, friends, community of faith, or others in their support networks.

As the seizure counselor, you will guide your patients through painful moments to support their growing independence and self-esteem, and to challenge their inner blocks to reaching their optimal potential.

How Do the Patient, Physician, and Seizure Counselor Work Together in the Process of "Taking Control"?

The process of "taking control" of seizures is a learning experience, similar to going to school or learning how to swim. The physician and seizure counselor work with the patient to guide her through the process of learning positive ways to cope with seizures. But like other learning situations, if the patient does not complete homework assignments, she will not assimilate session material. In this process of "taking control," the responsibility for making the effort, and learning new skills and applying them, is the patient's.

If the patient develops an understanding of his seizures as something to learn about over time, and from these new insights can cope more effectively with seizures and stressors, he has made an important start. If he decides to work with this approach, his *Workbook* will serve as a resource to guide him through the process of "taking control." This will include teaching him how his thoughts, moods, physical reactions, behaviors, and environment influence his life experiences; understanding how these aspects affect his seizures and how his doctor and possibly medication can help will enable him to cope and live a fulfilling life, even with his seizures.

Review with the patient *Workbook* Figure 1.1 (Five Aspects of Your Life Experiences).

Setting Treatment Expectations

Most people who are motivated to undertake an in-depth program such as this one are among the many individuals with seizures that are not well-controlled with medications. Central nervous system medications alone rarely fully control NES. Others, whose seizures are partially controlled with medication, undertake this program because they want to minimize medication dosage and drug side effects and to improve the quality of their lives. Of those individuals who complete this program, many will be able to stop their seizures altogether, through a combination of medication, lifestyle changes, and psychological work. For others, because of the nature of their particular kind of seizures, eliminating all seizures will not occur.

What can occur and *is* possible for everyone who decides to go ahead with this program is a great improvement in her or his ability to cope with having seizures. While not all kinds of seizures are totally "controllable" in the sense of completely eliminating seizures, everyone can learn to control how seizures affect his or her life. This means that they have the possibility of reducing the negative effects of having seizures, while enhancing the positive effects of increased self-esteem and level of wellness. Despite having a chronic illness, patients can gain a sense of being "in control" of their seizures, of their lives, and of their well-being.

Beginning the Process of "Taking Control"

This first meeting with the patient will set the tone for all of the following sessions. It is during this initial appointment that "homework" is introduced and your expectations as therapist are firmly established. At the conclusion of this appointment ask your patients (1) to begin recording the number of seizures they have in their daily seizure diary (Seizure Log), and (2) to review with you the first assignment on distinguishing situations, moods, and thoughts, which may have been completed prior to or during the appointment (see *Workbook*, Chapter 1). Remind your patient to bring their *Workbook*, Journal and all paperwork to every appointment, preferably assembled in a three-ring binder to facilitate organization.

> ✓ **Clinician Note**
>
> *When conducting the introductory appointment, as outlined in the beginning of this chapter, some of the time during the appointment will be devoted to reviewing the patient's answers to the Worksheet.*

N.B. the patient should have completed the exercise entitled Distinguishing Situations, Moods, and Thoughts *and should have corrected it before arriving at the appointment. If he has not completed the exercise beforehand, have him complete it in appointment, and go over the answers during the appointment, noting any difficulties with his ability to make the distinctions.*

Exercise: Distinguishing Situations, Moods, and Thoughts

Worksheet 1 is an exercise designed to help patients better distinguish between their thoughts, moods, and situations.[2] The patient is instructed to write on the line at the right whether the item in the left column is a thought, mood, or situation. The first three items have been completed as examples in Box 2.1.

Following the "quiz" in the *Workbook* are answers to Worksheet 1. The patient is asked to check her responses and write the correct answer next to her original one and to review the pertinent sections of this chapter to clarify any differences between her own answers and the ones given. If patients have any difficulty distinguishing among situations, moods, and thoughts, they are encouraged to review them with you, as it is important to distinguish these parts of their experiences in order to make changes in their lives. By separating these components from each other, patients will be better able to make changes that are important to them.

Close this introductory appointment by asking if the patient has any questions, and inquire if the patient is ready to take on the next session. Asking the patient if he wants to do the next session, rather than

---

Box 2.1. Example of Worksheet 1: Distinguishing Situations, Moods, and Thoughts

Situation, Mood, or Thought?

1. Nervous. _____ *mood* _____ (3 response examples are provided in the *Workbook*)

2. At home. _____ *situation* _____

3. I'm not going to be able to do this. _____ *thought* _____

4. Sad. _____ *[patient starts his or her own answers here in Workbook]* _____

5. Talking to a friend on the phone. _____

6. Irritated. _____

From *Mind over Mood* by Dennis Greenberger and Christine A. Padesky. © 1995 The Guilford Press.

---

[2] The complete Exercise can be found in Chapter 1 of the *Workbook*.

simply assuming he does, is one of the communication methods used to develop the patient's internal locus of control. If he answers "Yes," give the instruction, "Ok. Complete the next *Workbook* session, front to back before your next appointment." Encourage the patient to "mark it up," and write responses to all questions on the pages.

✓ **Clinician Note**

When you assign a Workbook *session to your patient, it is important to emphasize that the patient should read each session fully, prior to the next scheduled visit, and complete all exercises, writing down any questions to discuss in the upcoming appointment.*

Workbook Chapter 2, entitled "Session 1: Making the Decision to Begin the Process of Taking Control," outlines each step of the process, so that the patient will be fully aware of what is involved. At the close of the appointment, you can briefly highlight the next session assignment, noting that the patient will need to prepare a list of reasons that she wants to "take control" and reasons that she does not. Emphasize that it is critical for the patient to answer the question, "Do I want to begin the process of taking control?"

Challenging or Problematic Responses

Although there is a general acceptance of common psychiatric diagnoses among patients (i.e., a patient accepts a depression or anxiety diagnosis), some patients might have difficulty accepting the NES diagnosis. They might feel that they are being told that their problems are "all in her (or his) head" or that their symptoms are being "faked." It is critical to define NES in a clear manner as real, but not epileptic, in order to ensure from the outset that the patient has a complete understanding of the diagnosis and its implications.

However, from the start, it is important not to *convince* a patient that he has a diagnosis. If he does not buy into the diagnosis, he will resist the treatment. Also, do not convince a patient that he should enroll in treatment. If you convince him to enroll, you are setting up the dynamic at the outset that you will be working harder than he will be. You do not need to be a salesman for treatment. If a patient shows resistance or gives numerous reasons that he cannot or will not do therapy, let him know that it sounds like this may not be the best time for him and that if he finds that he needs it, or his seizures continue, he has your number and can contact you to set up an appointment.

✓ **Clinician Note**

Throughout this Therapist Guide *we provide examples of occasional problems that we have encountered with patient/seizure counselor interactions. In some instances, these examples illustrate maladaptive statements that a patient has made and how to address these statements. In other instances, we provide examples of erroneous statements that a seizure counselor has made, and we correct these statements.*

CHAPTER 3

Session 1: Making the Decision to Begin the Process of Taking Control

(Corresponds to *Workbook* Chapter 2)

MATERIALS NEEDED/TASKS

- Seizure Log (one completed from prior days and one blank for future days)
- Journal
- Patient's completed Session 1, "Making the Decision to Begin the Process of Taking Control"
- Patient to identify a support person prior to the next appointment
- Session 2: "Getting Support," to assign at end of appointment

APPOINTMENT OUTLINE

- Briefly outline the treatment sessions overview.
- Introduce the process of "taking control."
- Discuss GOAT session structure (Goals, Obstacles, Assignments, and Tools).
- Review Seizure Log elements.
- Signature "ceremony."
- Assign homework: Session 2.

OVERVIEW

- **Goal:** In Session 1 the main goal is for the patient to begin the process of "taking control" of his or her seizures.

- **Obstacle:** Having a fear of failure, avoidance of responsibility, and secondary gain are discussed as potential obstacles to good health.
- **Assignments:** The patient is instructed to complete a weekly Seizure Log and a journal, which includes a detailed description of what the patient was doing and feeling prior to, during, and following a seizure.
- **Tools:** A frank discussion with the patient about motivation and obstacles as the patient weighs the pros and cons of undergoing treatment.

✓ **Clinician Note: Appointment Structure**

A general structure for the appointments that helps to focus the patient and provide a framework is to:

1. *Start with an open-ended introduction, such as, "How are things?"*
2. *Review Seizure Log, journal, and last goal chosen by patient.*
3. *Read aloud the current Session Goal.*
4. *Review any Obstacles to accomplish session Goal selected by patient.*
5. *Review contents/concepts of chapter and areas highlighted by patient.*
6. *Review completed Assignments/Tools.*
7. *Brief preview of next session, which is given with instruction to complete it.*
8. *Confirm next appointment date and time.*

Therapist Behaviors

The primary goal of Session 1 is to guide the patient through the pros and cons of undergoing treatment for NES. The goal of this treatment is not to "cure" NES but rather to teach the patient strategies for better seizure management in order to live a richer life. You will explain that "taking control of seizures" means learning how to recognize that life's ups and downs can impact seizure activity and one's health in general. Many people with seizures adopt an "illness identity" and begin attributing all their difficulties in life to their seizures. During this appointment you will help the patient to answer the question, "Are you going to allow your disorder to control you, or do you choose to develop as a person and take control of your life and well-being?" This is what is meant by "making the decision to take control."

After this introduction, provide a brief overview of the treatment sessions (given in the Workbook *and summarized below) in order to provide a preview of how one learns to take control of her or his life.* Each session is designed to be covered in one visit (or more, if needed for mastery) with the seizure counselor. Between appointments, you will ask your patients to make observations about relevant aspects of their lives, to write about assigned topics in their journals, and to keep Seizure Logs. With some sessions, you will ask your patients to practice a given exercise dealing with self-observation or relaxation on a daily basis in their own homes/environments. You will also emphasize that each week at the end of the appointment, you will assign your patients the next session with the instruction to read the next chapter, or "session," and to write pertinent information in their *Workbook* in preparation for the next appointment with you.

Each session has a specific focus that builds on the prior session and covers the specific material. The sessions are summarized, as follows:

Summary of the Sessions

Introduction: Introduction for the Patient

In this introduction, patients receive an overview of important concepts related to the treatment, including aspects of the patient's life experience and the differentiation of situations, thoughts, and moods.

Session 1: Making the Decision to Begin the Process of Taking Control

In Session 1, patients will look in depth at what this treatment has to offer and will explore motivating factors and obstacles to taking control of their seizures. At the end of this session, the patient will make the decision whether or not to begin this work with a seizure counselor.

Session 2: Getting Support

Many people who begin this process lack the supportive relationships they need and often feel isolated and lonely. This session offers skills to help patients avoid isolation, improve communication, and to develop positive relationships with others.

Session 3: Deciding About Your Drug Therapy

Schedule this appointment to include the seizure counselor, the patient, and the patient's physician (if available to call in). This step encourages the patient to discuss and decide jointly what level of medication will be most beneficial while undertaking this "taking control" program. While too little medication may result in more frequent seizures if the patient has epilepsy (followed by periods when it is difficult to communicate or to think clearly), too much medication may leave the patient drowsy, confused, or unable to remember what was read or discussed at the last counseling appointment. Session 3 is the patient's opportunity for a "team conference" to determine the most beneficial drug regimen and to clear up any questions that he or she may have about anticonvulsant drug therapy.

Session 4: Learning to Observe Your Triggers

In this session the patient learns how to recognize factors that often trigger seizures. Common examples include situations leading to an emotional state of excitement or frustration, skipping medications, or overusing alcohol or drugs. In Session 4, patients will begin to identify and observe their own triggers, in order to eventually enable patients to reduce the frequency of their seizures.

Session 5: Channeling Negative Emotions Into Productive Outlets

The triggers observed in Session 4 usually lead to seizures because they first produce a negative emotion, such as fear, anger, or hurt. Session 5 provides skills for dealing positively with negative states, through expression, self-acceptance, and seeing a negative state as a demand for action.

Session 6: Relaxation Training: Experiencing the Sensation of the Brain Changing Itself

This session offers a large variety of different methods and skills that people find effective for reducing tension and achieving relaxation. These methods can potentially offer greater control over seizures, as well as enhance physical and psychological health.

Session 7: Identifying Your Pre-Seizure Aura

The pre-seizure aura consists of a symptom or sensation that precedes a seizure. Learning to identify an aura is an important step because the aura will enable the patient to take control by preventing seizures and/or avoiding injury or embarrassment.

Session 8: Dealing With External Life Stresses

"Dealing with life stresses" means both gaining awareness of the stressful factors in the patient's life and taking responsibility for relieving those factors that are within the patient's control. With long-term efforts, this process can have a dramatic impact on reducing seizure frequency and increasing well-being.

Session 9: Dealing With Internal Issues and Conflicts

The feelings, conflicts, and issues that are part of a person's inner being affect overall health as much or more than external stresses do. Examples include feelings of inadequacy, constantly blaming others for one's difficulties, and chronic states of anxiety or depression. Becoming aware of these issues and learning to deal with them is the focus of in-depth therapy, which some individuals who reach Session 9 decide to undertake with their seizure counselor or another trained therapist.

Session 10: Enhancing Personal Wellness

Wellness includes all the lifestyle choices that affect bodily health, and extends beyond the physical, into the realm of emotion, spirit, and meaning. This session allows the patient to move toward an optimum level of wellness by reviewing past successes in coping with seizures and assisting the patient to make new goals for ongoing self-care.

Session 11: Other Symptoms Associated With Seizures

"Other seizure symptoms" include altered states such as déjà vu, out-of-body experiences, memory problems and scattered thinking, as well as behavioral symptoms such as a slowing of activity or sudden outbursts of anger. The goal of Session 11 is to recognize, accept, and cope positively with "other seizure symptoms."

Taking Control: An Ongoing Process

Now that treatment is ending, it is up to the patient to determine how to continue the ongoing process of taking control. You will emphasize that your patient plays an important part in his or her continued growth and ability to live life to the fullest.

CASE VIGNETTE SUMMARY

Taking Control: An Example

Key aspects of the vignette cases are summarized in this Therapist Guide, *while the complete cases appear in the Patient* Workbook.

Mike began having seizures at age 19 while he was in college. Because of his seizures, he stopped college and moved back with his parents. For the next five years, he did not work or go to school and continued to have seizures despite taking three or four medications. He was seen by several experts, who recommended increasing his anticonvulsant medicines.

Mike wanted to be on less medication because he felt tired all the time, and it was hard to think clearly. At this point Mike started to work with a seizure counselor. He learned about his pre-seizure aura (an unpleasant smell), triggers to his seizures, and relaxation methods. His seizure counselor told him he needed to take control of his life if he wanted to have a chance to reduce the frequency of his seizures. Mike decided he was ready to learn about his feelings and to get moving in his life. He began to write about his emotional reactions in his journal, and to talk openly about his feelings with his seizure counselor. He got a job as a volunteer and started taking classes at a local college. He continued to have seizures, but less often.

Then he decided not to let his seizures prevent him from having an active social life. He began to go out with friends he met at college and developed a close relationship with a girlfriend. He found her to be understanding and supportive when he discussed his seizures. Despite the fact that his seizures continued, he had become so competent at his volunteer job that he was offered a paying job at the same office where he had been a volunteer. He and his girlfriend decided to get married. Over the next year he learned to recognize tensions in his life that created the type of feelings that preceded his seizures. He was able to talk about his feelings before the tensions got out of hand. He also exercised regularly. He looked and felt more relaxed. His seizures came under control—he was still taking three medications—and after two years without seizures he finally got a driver's license. Mike took control of his life; his seizures no longer controlled his life.

Introduce the Goals, Obstacles, Assignments, and Tools (GOAT) *Workbook* Structure

Goal

Throughout the *Workbook*, each session will contain a goal that summarizes the patient's work for that particular step. *In each appointment, read the session goal aloud with the patient.*

The goal of the first session is to make the decision to begin the process of taking control.

Obstacles

For every step, there will also be a discussion of some of the obstacles that other people have had to overcome in order to achieve their goals. This discussion of obstacles helps to acknowledge that the step the patient is trying to take is not easy. Your job is to normalize that it is "OK" to feel unsure and ambivalent about going ahead with the process of "taking control." Your patient should select the obstacles (shown in the *Workbook* and below) to accomplishing the goal. Use what the patient selected as launch points for discussion in the appointment.

The following list includes some of the most frequent obstacles that people with seizures experience as they make the decision to begin the process of taking control:

- Not wanting responsibility (preferring to be taken care of by family members and to have one's doctor take all the responsibility for seizure control)
- Fear of failure
- Wanting to avoid going out into the world
- Wanting to continue being the center of attention (because of seizures, inability to drive, etc.)
- Wishing to maintain control over one's family (Some families treat members with seizures as special or fragile, allowing the individual with seizures to have his or her way much of the time.)
- Afraid of losing help from family and friends.

CASE VIGNETTE SUMMARY

Obstacles: An Example

When Maggie was first seen at age 14 by a neurologist, she communicated like an 8- or 9-year-old child. She had had partial-complex seizures from early childhood. Her generalized, or "grand-mal," seizures were controlled with two anticonvulsant medications, but she continued to have up to 12 complex partial seizures every day. At school she stayed to herself and felt odd and left out. At home she spent most of her time acting angry and surly with her father. She made it clear that she was very unhappy—and in her mind, her seizures and her father were to blame. At her physician's suggestion, Maggie started to work with a seizure counselor. In her first sessions, she began to express some of her anger more openly. She was able to see how much she blamed her father and her seizures for everything she did not like about her life. As time went on, she began to reach out and develop friendships at school—to plan some social activities after school and on weekends that she really enjoyed. The first step to taking control for Maggie was to stop blaming, and to start taking some responsibility for making her life better, which were her main obstacles to taking control of her seizures.

Tool

Each session will offer the patient a new "tool" toward taking control. These tools include a variety of methods for self-observation, self-awareness, and changing patterns of behavior. As your patients practice these methods in the office setting and at home, they will discover and incorporate these tools into their lives.

Often the *Workbook* will ask the patient to prepare for a particular discussion or activity for the upcoming appointment. The patient will be expected to fill in all *Workbook* sections as they are read, as well as to complete the assignments at the end of the previous chapter.

The "tool" for helping your patients make a decision about whether or not to undertake intensive work with a seizure counselor will be a discussion of all the positive and negative feelings about beginning this process of "taking control." Before coming in for the office visit, patients are asked to make a list of their obstacles, as well as the reasons that they are motivated to go ahead and make the decision to begin the process of taking control.

Tool: In-Office Discussion

The tool for accomplishing the goal of Session 1 is a discussion of the motivating factors and obstacles the patient has listed. This will give the patient an opportunity to become more aware of his or her own feelings, as well as to begin a process of honest communication between the patient, the patient's physician, and the seizure counselor.

At the end of this discussion, ask the patient to make a decision about whether or not they want to begin the process of taking control. If the answer is "Yes," arrange a schedule for regular counseling appointments and answer any questions the patient has about the treatment program. If the answer is "No," the patient will have the option of continuing to see their physician for seizure medications and necessary lab tests but will be choosing not to undertake the intensive time-limited program for taking control of their seizures outlined in the *Workbook*. The option to engage in the treatment in the future when the patient is ready should be offered.

For some people who recognize the challenges presented in a program such as this one, the decision about whether they want to undertake it is not an easy one. Many patients experience a kind of inner "war" for and against going ahead with such a major life decision. It is helpful if you discuss the patient's identified pros and cons (i.e., motivating factors and obstacles) in order to help the patient make an informed decision based on what the patient wants versus what the patient's doctor or family might want.

The Signature "Ceremony"

Whether or not the patient has decided to "take control" and accept treatment for NES, it is helpful to have them sign a "contract" regarding this decision. You will emphasize, *"What you are signing here is like a contract. This contract is with yourself. You are not doing this for me, or for a husband/wife, or your children or anyone else. This choice and this work are from you and for you.*"

DO I WANT TO BEGIN THIS PROCESS OF TAKING CONTROL?

Yes _____ No _____ Signature _____ Date _____

After a patient lists motivations and obstacles and agrees to treatment (provided agreement is the outcome), advise your patient,

> *As you work through the upcoming sessions, some of the material can be challenging. If that occurs with you, you can refer back to this time when you made the deal with yourself, and you can review what you have listed here to remind yourself of why you are doing this hard work.*

Assignments

Seizure Log

The Seizure Log is a daily record of seizure activity, which the patient records on the forms located at the end of each *Workbook* session. Ask your patient to keep careful records of seizure frequency on these log sheets throughout the entire process, as well as during the 3 to 9 months following completion of this "taking control" program, so they can do a 1-year comparison.

The purpose of the Seizure Log is to provide the patient, the seizure counselor, and the patient's physician with an accurate record of how often seizures occur. In this way, the patient will be able to chart progress and to learn what methods are effective in helping to decrease the frequency of seizures. Because these Seizure Logs are a learning tool in this process of "taking control," it is essential that the patient fills them out accurately on a daily basis. The patient may wish to make copies of the Seizure Log forms or record seizures in her journal.

Instruct your patient, beginning with this week, to record the following information on the Seizure Log form provided in the *Workbook:*

- **Number of seizures**: At the end of each day, record how many seizures you had that day. Put a "0" if you did not have any seizures to document that day.

- **Time(s) of day**: Write what time of the day the seizure(s) occurred.
- **Duration(s)**: Record approximately how long the seizure lasted. You may want to consult a family member or another person who witnessed the seizure about how long the seizure lasted.
- **Description(s)**: Record what symptoms you experienced with the seizure, before, during and after the event. If you were unaware of the event, how did others describe it? Again, consult anyone who witnessed the seizure for assistance in describing what happened to you when you had the seizure.
- **Location(s)**: Record where you were when the seizure occurred. Be as specific as you can.
- **Severity (1: mild, 2: moderate, 3: severe)**: Use the numbers for the following terms (mild, moderate, severe) to rate the severity of the seizure.
- **Trigger(s)**: Record what occurred *right before your seizure*. Any action, emotion, thought, or experience can be listed as a trigger. Be as specific as possible. For instance, instead of just writing "stress," record the specific stressful event, emotion, or thought.
- **Precursor(s)**: Record what was happening during the day. Any event, situation, or mood in the time leading up to the seizure can be a precursor. You can think of this as the "climate" for the day.
- **Improved with**: Record how you recovered from your seizure. What made the seizure stop?
- **Impact on your day**: Record how the seizure affected the rest of your day.
- **Impact on others**: Record how the seizure, or your recovery, affected those around you, including witnesses, or other family or friends.

Ask the patient if he or she requires clarification of any questions regarding the Seizure Logs.

Journal-Keeping

Journal-keeping is a very important part of this "taking control" program. Writing in a journal will constitute a valuable portion of the patient's weekly assignments as they progress through the sessions in the *Workbook*. After making the decision to begin the process of taking control, your patient will need to obtain or purchase a notebook (such as a spiral-bound notebook) or a blank bound book to use as their own personal journal.

What Is the Purpose of Keeping a Journal, and How Will It Help the Patient?

Writing on a regular basis in a journal will help patients notice and express thoughts and feelings. You should emphasize that the journal is a safe, personal space for patients to write about themselves and their lives, their experiences, their progress, their aspirations, their loves, hates, times of happiness, and times of loneliness and sorrow. It is a sanctuary where the patient can answer the question: "How do I really feel about this?"

Connecting feelings and reactions is an integral part of the patient's work with you. However, the journal is a private place for patients to explore their inner selves. Patients should not feel that they *have* to show anyone what they have written in their journals unless the patient decides that they want to read a particular section to someone whom they trust, including you. They might choose to share entries in seeking understanding and support for their feelings, or to ask you to help them gain insight into their own emotional responses. But the weekly journal-keeping assignments that are given in the *Workbook*—as well as the daily entries that patients may make about their lives and reactions—remain their personal province.

Once your patient develops the habit of writing regularly in his journal, it will become a reliable resource for self-discovery. It will provide them with the opportunity to ask themself questions, to let go of feelings, to explore preoccupations and powerful emotional responses. It will allow them to observe and understand their behavior and motivations. In particular, they will gain insight into how their life experiences affect their seizures and overall well-being. It will provide reminders of the things that they are learning as they participate in this therapy. It will become an increasingly valuable tool for taking control of their seizures and their life. Asking if there is an entry they want to discuss is fine and is encouraged, and they may do so at some point.

In addition to making daily entries in the journal about personal events and emotional responses, this week's journal-keeping assignment is to *write a detailed description in your journal of what you did and felt before, during, and after a seizure.*

If your patient does not experience a seizure this week, encourage them to complete this assignment after they have their next seizure or from a recent prior seizure.

Identify a Support Person Before the Next Appointment

A support person is someone whom the patient chooses to help give support throughout this process of "taking control." The support person can be a family member, friend, or spouse. The patient should choose someone they trust and know well, and who will be available on a regular basis over the next 3–6 months.

> ✓ **Clinician Note**
>
> *Occasionally, a person with seizures does not have anyone he or she feels comfortable identifying as a support person. In these instances, encourage your patient to talk with you about options for identifying a support person. Other people may include a counselor, a pastor, or a trustworthy member of his or her community.*

End of the Appointment

Try to incorporate any substantive questions raised by the patient before the final moments of the current appointment when closing with info on the next session review statement and scheduling next appointment. Doing so models bringing time and conversations to closure for appropriate social interactions and limits the "oh, by the way . . ." statements, as a patient is exiting. The social-psychological-interpersonal structure provided in appointments can then generalize to promote structure in patients' lives outside the treatment office room.

For many patients, this will be the first time they have been given "homework" in therapy. Be sensitive to this fact, and acknowledge that this is a different kind of therapy. To illustrate that coming to the appointments is not enough, you can use a school analogy such as, "If you were taking a new class in school and you always attended the class but never completed the homework assignments, you would not effectively learn the material."

- Patient (P): "I don't know what to write. What belongs in a journal? I have never done a journal in my life. Do I write how many times I went to the bathroom, or how I feel?"
- Seizure counselor (SC): "In the journal you can explore your inner self."
- P: "I don't even know what that means."
- SC: "It's kind of an exploration. There's no way you can do this wrong." (Give examples of what to write, such as a simple daily entry on an activity or idea.)
- P: "Well, I've never done it, so I don't know where to begin."
- SC: "If you are having trouble, start with simple things. 'It's raining today. I have a headache. I had a nice dinner with my sister.' Just putting everyday things down on paper is a great start."

Seizure Logs

Two copies of the Seizure Log are included at the end of every session in the *Workbook*. Encourage full completion each week.

CHAPTER 4

Session 2: Getting Support

(Corresponds to *Workbook* Chapter 3)

MATERIALS NEEDED/TASKS

- Seizure Log
- Journal
- Goal-setting
- Patient's completed Session 2: "Getting Support"
- Session 3: "Deciding About Your Drug Therapy," to assign at end of appointment

APPOINTMENT OUTLINE

- Review homework assigned in the previous appointment.
- Review reading exercises.
- Discuss the importance of "getting support" as part of the "taking control" process.
- Identify obstacles to "getting support."
- Review passive, aggressive, and assertive communication styles.
- Review accomplishment of (or barrier to) a small, realistic, action-oriented goal.
- Assign homework: Session 3.

OVERVIEW

As noted in the introduction to this *Therapist Guide*, at the conclusion of each appointment, instruct your patient to read and complete the *Workbook* session for the next appointment. During the appointment, your role as therapist is to review the work and assignments that the patient completed, discuss any obstacles to completion of that work, and address any patient questions or concerns.

- **Goal:** In Session 2 the principal goal is for the patient to begin the process of "getting support" from the people to whom the patient feels close in order to have help in the process of "taking control."
- **Obstacle:** The patient identifies potential obstacles to "getting support," including rejection sensitivity, anger, difficulty asking for help, viewing asking for help as a sign of "weakness," and social anxiety.
- **Assignments:** Instruct the patient to continue with the seizure log and journal, as well as to complete a small social goal he or she identified in the chapter session.
- **Tools:** You can help your patients identify their communication styles in order to help them learn to improve communication skills. Instruct the patient to choose a small, realistic, action-oriented social goal to complete before the next appointment.

Therapist Behaviors

In Session 2, you will be emphasizing the importance of building a social support network. Having seizures can lead to insular behavior, as well as a loss of support from friends and family. This can happen because people without seizures may be frightened or put off by seizures and because people with seizures themselves may be uncomfortable about how others will react and therefore avoid socializing. Research has shown that "friends are good medicine," and that people who have regular contact with friends have higher levels of physical and mental health than people without much contact with friends.

Session 2 focuses on teaching skills that will help the patient avoid loneliness and to obtain positive support from others. Because isolation and difficulty getting along with others often result from poor communication, this session emphasizes the skills needed for communicating effectively with others. After you address potential obstacles to socialization, identify the patient's communication style (i.e., passive communication, aggressive communication, and assertive communication). Passive and aggressive communications are unhealthy communication styles that may contribute to the erosion of relationships.

Assist your patient in reviewing the small, realistic, action-oriented goals they identified, which will aid in improving relationships, making friends, improving communication skills, and finding a partner. Learning to set small, realistic goals that the patient can succeed at each week will create a sense of accomplishment that will lead to addressing larger goals, such as "taking control."

Getting Support

In Session 1, patients took the first major step in making the decision to "take control" of their seizures. That step may be the first in a series in the process of gaining control over their lives. Part of "taking control" is to build and strengthen relationships by "getting support." "Getting support" means asking for help and encouragement when patients need it and expressing feelings openly to the people they feel close to. It means developing relationships with family members and friends in whom they feel accepted and supported in their efforts to take control of their lives. Because relationships are mutual, this means accepting others and offering support to them in return. *Review the name of the person that the patient designated as a support person and why that person was chosen.*

Loneliness is a widespread problem in our society, and people with seizures often experience it severely. Seizures are *not* the cause of loneliness or social isolation, but they can certainly contribute to it. This happens both because other people may be frightened or put off by seizures, and because people with seizures themselves may be uncomfortable about how others will react and therefore avoid socializing. Some individuals with seizures also find that the few close relationships they do have are full of anger and resentment both within and from others, in part because of the frustration that can result from dealing with the seizure disorder itself.

If your patient feels rejected and angry with people he wants to be close to, he is missing important support for coping with seizures. He also lacks support if he does not have close friends with whom he can talk openly.

Read the session goal from the Workbook *aloud with the patient.*

Goal

The goal of this session is for the patient to obtain the support he needs for the process of taking control.

Obstacles

Obstacles to obtaining social support can be numerous. Assist the patient in identifying possible obstacles by reviewing and discussing the obstacles that the patient selected in the *Workbook*. The list begins with:

- Blaming the patient's family or doctor.
- Feeling hurt or rejected by others.
- Seeing family and friends as responsible for taking care of the patient.
- Poor memory, which interferes with social interactions.
- Not feeling able to ask for emotional support.
- Other: (an open space is there for the patient to fill in, for any unidentified obstacle)

Tools

Tool #1: Improving Communication Skills

Introduce a model of communication that divides communication styles into three categories: passive, aggressive and assertive. Examples of the three communication styles are included in the *Workbook*. The patient will have written their own examples for discussion.

Passive communication occurs when a person avoids expressing personal needs directly and often leads to situations where that person feels resentful. The passive communicator expresses feelings, sometimes nonverbally as pouting or resentful avoidance, and sometimes with an angry outburst when a series of these situations have built up. The result is poor communication, unspoken resentment, and unsupportive relationships with the people most needed for support.

Aggressive communication is characterized by verbal attacks that blame or threaten other people in order to get what is wanted. Aggressive communication often leads to situations where the other person feels pushed around and in turn avoids or rejects the aggressive person.

The aggressive communicator (in the case included in the *Workbook*, the wife) began with an accusation (a "you" message) and the situation went from bad to worse. This type of accusing, demanding statement is quite common between people and almost always leads to a situation where nobody wins. Aggressive communication has the disadvantage that it leads to subsequent interactions that also result in mutual attack—resulting in a relationship with diminished possibilities for warmth and support.

Assertive communication is the healthy form of communication and involves expressing feelings honestly and standing up for oneself over issues that are personally important. It includes respect for the other person's feelings and opinions, while at the same time respecting oneself and one's own needs. Assertive communication conveys the feeling that you care about the other person and the relationship enough to try to express what you want as clearly as possible.

In the assertive communication example in the *Workbook*, the assertive communicator used clear, "I" messages, such as, "I'd like you to help me" and "I feel angry when. . . ." These messages strongly convey both the communicator's need for help and the angry feelings that resulted when the other person was unwilling to do what was asked. There was also a statement, "I know you don't like to be interrupted," which acknowledged the other person's feelings. The assertive communicator stood up for her own needs and feelings and also indicated a willingness to modify the original request in order to take into account her husband's wishes.

The result was that the assertive communicator got what she wanted: to get the job done through joint participation and shared responsibility for the chore. In addition, trust was enhanced between the two people because they were able to solve an interpersonal problem in a way that neither person felt blamed or taken advantage of. This kind of healthy assertive communication, which may be used in talking about household chores and responsibilities or about more personal needs for recognition or affection, is useful in building the kind of relationships that meet our basic human needs for caring and support.

Communication Style Exercise

As noted in the *Workbook*, the patient was instructed to complete an exercise in preparation for this appointment, which asked the patient to provide examples of her own style of passive, aggressive, and assertive communication, and what resulted from these examples. If there is not enough time to review all of these examples, select a few to use as a point of discussion. Ask the patient which style she uses most. Ask to assign a percentage for how much she uses each style. If she is using the unhealthy forms (passive, aggressive), ask how that affects her relationships. Ask if she is interested in changing from unhealthy forms of communication to healthy assertive communication and if she can incorporate the healthy form (assertive) in her communication with others. Review any obstacles to using healthy assertive communication. Encourage practice.

✓ **Clinician Note**

The challenge with the regressive/passive patient is that when trying to provide needed structure, you may inadvertently take on a paternalistic role, further reinforcing the infantilized position and the external locus of control that the patient exhibits. To balance this potential, as soon as structure is explained, you can "put the ball in the court" of the patient by asking, "So what do you think you need to do next?" Or simply, "OK, nice work. What do you propose next?"

Tool #2: Goal-Setting

Help your patient with the process of identifying small, realistic, action-oriented goals, which will aid in improving relationships, making friends, improving communication skills, and finding a partner.

Learning to set small, realistic goals that the patient can succeed at each week will create a sense of accomplishment that will lead to developing agency, and addressing larger goals, such as "taking control."

Most people have experienced frustration sometime in the past with setting goals for themselves that are too difficult to accomplish, leading to disappointment and a sense of failure. You can help your patients set goals by choosing goals which have the following characteristics:

1. **Small is beautiful.** Small goals are goals that can really be met. They give a person a well-deserved feeling of personal satisfaction from his accomplishments. The accumulation of many small, successfully accomplished goals can lead to big changes in one's life, as well as increased confidence and self-esteem.

2. **Realistic is essential.** A realistic goal is a goal that the patient will really be able to complete in one week, despite all the demands of the patient's life.

3. **Action-oriented goals are doable, whereas feeling-oriented goals are not.** Very often, the patient will not be able to meet a goal that deals with his emotions, such as "to feel relaxed when I have dinner with my parents this week." But the patient *can* choose to do some action that he has complete control over, such as deciding that after having dinner with his parents this coming week, he will write in his journal about his feelings. Or he will call his best friend and talk about his reactions. These are action-oriented goals that can help the patient cope with feelings, get support, and be successful in completing the goals he has set.

4. **Avoid thinking in *shoulds/coulds*.** Choosing to phrase goals positively rather than negatively is another tool that can help to focus energy on what it is the patient wants to do, rather than on what the patient does not want to do.

In preparation for this week's appointment, the patient selected ONE small, realistic, action-oriented goal related to Session 2 from the list of suggestions provided in the *Workbook*. Categories include the following:

- Improving relationships
- Making friends
- Improving communication skills
- If you are single (and do not want to be)

Review the goal the patient chose, and how the patient did or did not accomplish the goal. If she chose several goals, ask her to choose only one goal the next time. If she did not select any goal or could not accomplish one, discuss what barriers presented that hindered her.

✓ **Clinician Note**

To conclude and review, the structure of the session provides a framework for the treatment process and content. During the appointment, you and the patient will have discussed the prior assigned work.

Review Patient's In-Office Discussion Work

Review the patient's in-office discussion paperwork, including examples of passive, aggressive, and assertive communication, the patient's experience while having a seizure, and communication skills and barriers.

Review of Completed Assignments

When reviewing the patient's in-office discussion work, review the patient's completed homework assignments.

Seizure Log

Review the Seizure Log to assess frequency from the prior week, and discuss with your patient if he is able to identify any triggers or patterns. Let the patient make the associations.

Journal-Keeping

Give the patient the opportunity to discuss her journal topic description of what she did and felt before, during, and after a seizure. This discussion will be helpful for you and for the patient's support person to learn as much as you can about the patient's experience of having seizures.

Goal-Setting

From Tool #2 Goal List, the *Workbook* instructed the patient to select one goal for this week. Review with the patient the completion (or lack thereof) of the goal that the patient thought would help her to get more support from family members and/or friends.

"My goal for the week ending (give date) _____ is:"

The *Workbook* instructed the patient to write in the following information to show you in today's appointment:

"On _____ (give date), I tried to meet this goal with the following results:"

"I consider that I did _____/did not _____ meet the goal that I set for myself this week."

Review of Obstacles to Session 2

Discuss any obstacles to obtaining social support that the patient identified in the workbook exercise.

Review the Patient's Answers to the Questions Asked in the *Workbook*

Prior to this appointment, patients were assigned to write down responses and concerns, both as they read through the material on their own and later when they talk about these questions with you in the office.

Topic #1: The Patient's Experience of Having Seizures

1. How the patient feels about having seizures in front of other people.
2. Factors that the patient and support person have noticed that seem to bring on seizures.
3. Sensations the patient has that precede seizures (i.e., aura).

4. How the patient's seizures look to another person, such as the support person.

5. Is the patient's experience similar to or different from other people who have seizures?

6. Any other observations, questions, or concerns that the patient or the patient's support person wants to bring up.

Topic #2: Communication Skills and Barriers

Provide your patient the opportunity to discuss both positive and negative experiences in relation to you and/or the support person by the patient answering the following questions:

1. What are some recent examples where the patient felt communication between you and the patient or the patient and support person was particularly good and/or especially bad or difficult?

2. Is there anything you or the support person said that the patient did not like?

3. In what ways does the patient need help and support in the process of taking control?

Preparing for the Next Appointment

- After completing this session, instruct the patient to read and complete "Session 3: Deciding About Your Drug Therapy" in preparation for the next appointment.

- Also instruct your patient to contact his or her prescribing physician to let the doctor know that the patient will be discussing medications with you and making important decisions regarding the medications the physician prescribes for the patient. The patient can let the prescribing doctor know that she or he can contact you with any pertinent information. You and the patient can let the prescribing doctor know that he or she can call in to the next appointment on medication therapy, if he or she desires.

Some patients might feel overwhelmed by the process of "taking control" given that it requires motivation and sustained concentration and effort. It is important to acknowledge that the program is intensive, yet to not reinforce the idea that "not feeling well" is a reason for not doing the work. For many patients with NES, "not feeling well" has led to enabling behavior from family members (i.e., taking over the patient's responsibilities). One consequence of this is that the patient can inadvertently internalize this message, which can lead to a self-fulfilling prophecy, resulting in the development of a "sick" identity and illness behaviors. Taking control means shedding the sick role. Rather than:

- P: "There are days I didn't feel like doing the work."
- SC: "Did you have a chance to think about why you didn't do it?"
- P: "No, I felt tired and shaky."
- SC: "It's not something you have to do every day of the week; if you are feeling well, do some of the work over time."

The seizure counselor in the above exchange could take a more directed approach to encourage healthy responses. Rather than accommodating to working when the patient feels better, consider reinforcing: "It can be difficult when you are tired. In this process of learning to take control of your seizures, those times when you are tired can be a time when you are also vulnerable to having symptoms. If you are able to train yourself to stay focused and do some work when you are tired, that may also apply to keeping control over the seizures. It is kind of like training for a marathon. Daily discipline gets the runner in shape. Does that make sense?"

Keep emphasizing, "For things to change for you, this has to be *your* work. I can facilitate the process as we review the work you have done when you bring it into the appointment."

Another issue that arises in discussion involves relationships.

- P: "My girlfriend is such a pain in the neck. She's always nagging about everything."
- SC: "You have a very difficult situation with your girlfriend. So you have to relearn the ways you are interacting with her and learn some new habits."

Try not to take sides, or even giving the appearance of doing so. In the appointment, you may be hearing only one side of the story, so you should avoid value-laden judgments on the patient's relationships. Overtly or inadvertently labeling other's behaviors negatively with "you have a difficult situation" may reinforce the patient's impressions or biases, which may be accurate or may be skewed.

An alternative approach is, "I see how that can be hard for you. Talk a bit more about how that affects you." This approach encourages the patient to identify internal states without the therapist siding with one party or another.

CHAPTER 5

Session 3: Deciding About Your Drug Therapy

(Corresponds to *Workbook* Chapter 4)

MATERIALS NEEDED/TASKS

- Seizure Log
- Journal
- Medication Log
- Patient's completed Session 3, "Deciding About Your Drug Therapy"
- Session 4, "Learning to Observe Your Triggers," to assign at end of appointment

APPOINTMENT OUTLINE

- Review homework assigned in the previous session.
- Review reading exercises.
- Identify obstacles the patient might have about communicating with his or her physician.
- Review medication material.
- Review accomplishment of (or barrier to) a small, realistic, action-oriented goal.
- Assign homework: Session 4.

OVERVIEW

Goal: The goal of Session 3 is for the patient to make a joint decision with his or her prescribing physician about current drug therapy (i.e., does it need to be increased, decreased, or discontinued?) before or while proceeding with Sessions 4 through the end of treatment.

Obstacle: Ask the patient to identify potential obstacles to addressing medications, including a lack of understanding about the benefits of anticonvulsant drug therapy, a lack of understanding about side effects, and a lack of communication with the prescribing physician.

Assignments: Instruct the patient to continue with the Seizure Log and journal, as well as to complete a small goal identified in the session list. Also, ask the patient to create a Medication Log list to record information about their medications.

Tools: In preparation for the appointment, the patient was instructed to read the written explanation of central nervous system (CNS) active medications. The patient was also instructed to invite his or her prescribing physician to call in to today's appointment, if available, to discuss medications. After the session content is discussed during the appointment, the patient is instructed to contact his or her prescribing physician in order to follow up about the discussion about their medications.

Therapist Behaviors

The goal of Session 3 is to guide the patient to work with the prescribing physician to make an informed decision about the patient's current medication regimen. Changes in a patient's medications might improve seizure control and boost intellectual and memory abilities. It is possible that a patient's medication side effects are interfering with his or her ability to participate in the "taking control" process. Adjusting medications might decrease seizure frequency and severity, thereby allowing the patient to participate in the "taking control" process more fully.

Patients with NES typically present on a combination of CNS medications, including antidepressants, anxiolytics, and anticonvulsant medications/antiepileptic drugs (AEDs). AEDs reduce the number and severity of epileptic seizures for a majority of people with epilepsy, *but AEDs do not treat NES*. Up to 80% of tonic-clonic (grand mal) epileptic seizures are controlled by AEDs, but less than 50% of complex partial epileptic seizures are totally controlled by AEDs. Moreover, research shows that AEDs may make NES worse. In addition, CNS medications can also cause disturbing side effects interfering with memory, cognitive abilities, alertness, personality, or mood.

Many people participating in this treatment program, particularly those with uncontrolled seizures, are taking such high doses of medications that they are experiencing drug side effects, such as memory loss and disruption of ability to think clearly or read. For individuals with lone NES (i.e., NES without epileptic seizures), it may be necessary to lower doses or taper and discontinue AEDs to enable the person to have sufficient mental clarity and psychological insight to use the *Workbook*, even if NES frequency increases slightly as a result. On the other hand, individuals with mixed epilepsy and NES (roughly 10% of patients with seizures) who are not on seizure drugs because they are opposed to taking any medication may need to consider low-dose AEDs for epilepsy and/or CNS medications for comorbid depression or anxiety, in order to reduce seizure frequency sufficiently to allow participation.

In our experience, patients derive great benefit from this medication discussion. Very often patients lack even basic knowledge about what they are putting in their bodies when they take medication. This discussion empowers patients to make informed decisions about their medications. In this chapter, patients will learn about pharmacologic interactions, how CNS medications reduce symptoms, basic facts about anticonvulsant drugs and how they work to reduce epileptic seizure activity, terms related to medications, about drug allergies, about lab tests for people taking anticonvulsant drugs, and about medication side effects. The goal is for your patients to be active participants in their medication decisions.

Below is a brief summary of the questions posed in the *Workbook* so you become familiar with the concepts and responses.

How Do Anticonvulsant Drugs Work to Reduce *Epileptic* Seizure Activity?

Anticonvulsants work by inhibiting neuronal excitation. By inhibiting the electrical activity of the brain, they act to decrease both the frequency and severity of epileptic seizures.

Antidepressants and anxiolytics may help with disorders associated with NES by treating comorbid symptoms of depression and anxiety or by modifying brain neurotransmitter levels. Mixed mechanism antidepressants work by both inhibiting and exciting different neuronal systems. Tricyclic antidepressants (TCAs) work by raising brain levels of norepinephrine. MAOIs, or monoamine oxidase inhibitors, work by raising levels of various neurotransmitters. Some AEDs are used as mood stabilizers or to prevent migraines or treat pain syndromes, as are TCAs. Benzodiazepines are also used for anxiety, and were described in the session material. Some medications that work on the adrenergic system, used for heart conditions (including beta-blockers or alpha-blockers), also treat headaches, anxiety, and symptoms of post-traumatic stress disorder (PTSD), which commonly occur in patients with NES.

Normal brain activity consists of two basic processes of "excitation" and "inhibition." Brain cells (neurons) communicate with each other all the time, signaling each other to fire (excitation) or to be quiet (inhibition). Figures are provided in the *Workbook* illustrating these concepts for the patients. With seizures, the balance between excitation and inhibition is upset in parts of the brain. Too much excitation occurs where neurons synchronously fire. This neuronal overexcitation manifests as an epileptic seizure. *In nonepileptic seizures, the abnormal neuronal firing found in epilepsy is not present.*

Many anticonvulsant drugs work in epileptic seizures to increase inhibition in damaged brain areas, theoretically preventing excessive excitation. On the other hand, if the medications cause too much inhibition of normal brain processes, side effects may occur.

Anticonvulsant medication effects may be specific to a specific *epileptic* seizure type. For years, phenytoin, carbamazepine, and phenobarbital were the mainstay of epilepsy treatment. These AEDs help control generalized tonic-clonic epileptic seizures, complex partial (focal) epileptic seizures, but not absence ("petit mal") epileptic seizures. Valproic acid is effective for what were referred to as "petit mal" absence epilepsy and other generalized epileptic seizures. Ethosuximide usually helps only

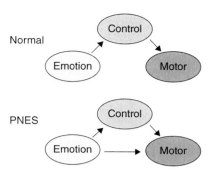

Figure 5.1

Psychogenic Nonepileptic Seizure Networks

Reproduced from van der Kruijs, et al., Functional connectivity of dissociation in patients with psychogenic non-epileptic seizures, *Journal of Neurology, Neurosurgery, and Psychiatry*, 83:239–247, © 2012, with permission from BMJ Publishing Group Ltd.

with "petit mal" absence epileptic seizures. There are a number of newer generation AEDs, which have specific indications for epilepsy types. The epilepsy type needs to be matched with the appropriate medication. In contrast to AEDs effects in epilepsy, *no anticonvulsant has been shown to effectively treat nonepileptic seizures.*

In contrast to epilepsy, NES has a different mechanism on the body, brain, and behavior. Epilepsy is reflected in the brain with abnormal neuronal firing. Abnormal neuronal firing does not occur in NES; rather, brain networks are thought to be disrupted (see Figure 5.1). The proposed brain network abnormalities do not "cause" NES, but may be a putative mechanism reflecting disruption of brain activity connections in some patients with NES in response to stressors and conflicts.

What Are Some Basic Facts the Patient Should Know About Anticonvulsant Drug Therapy?

Most people with epileptic seizures need to take an anticonvulsant drug. Quite often, a person with epilepsy will need to take medication every day for the rest of her life. A few individuals who experience seizures only at times of intense stress or during periods of substance abuse can control seizures without using medication.

Anticonvulsant drugs are not 100% effective in preventing epileptic seizures. Some people with epilepsy who take AEDs never have another seizure as long as they take their medicine regularly. Others, however, (at least 25% of people with seizures), continue to have some seizures on one or several anticonvulsant drugs.

Different people react differently to AEDs. A patient with epilepsy might have good results with a medication that is not effective in controlling someone else's seizures. Likewise, a patient might have a side effect from a drug that another person would not, and vice versa.

When a person takes an AED, his body gets used to having the medication in his bloodstream. His brain becomes sensitized to the effects of the drug, and if he stops taking the AED abruptly, his brain may react with severe withdrawal symptoms, such as prolonged severe epileptic seizures (*status epilepticus*), which can be life-threatening. Therefore, anticonvulsant drugs should be withdrawn slowly, by tapering the dose. Even if an AED is reduced slowly, the brain can still sense the withdrawal. A single withdrawal seizure is not reason to restart a particular medication. But for patients with epilepsy, if recurrent epileptic seizures occur after completely stopping a medication, restarting that AED or a similar one should be strongly considered. Fortunately, for patients with lone NES, research shows that AEDs can safely be tapered off without adverse events.

Patients with NES and no epilepsy who are taking an AED for an indication such as migraine prophylaxis or mood stabilization in bipolar disorder may continue to take AEDs, but the prescribing physician and seizure counselor should emphasize that the AED is not for NES.

What Basic Concepts Will Help Patients Understand Their Anticonvulsant Drug Therapy?

The *Workbook* contains information for patients on how medications work. Patients should read through the glossary of terms to familiarize themselves with the different medication concepts. Patients can refer to the glossary again when they read later material about the features of the particular anticonvulsant drugs or other CNS active agents that they are taking.

Glossary of Terms Relating to Medications

The *Workbook* glossary defines the following terms: blood levels, brand name, dosage, drug allergy, generic name, serum half-life, side effects, signs of toxicity, and therapeutic range.

Drug Information Tables

Your patient may still be taking an anticonvulsant, or she may have had the medication discontinued if her video EEG revealed lone NES (i.e., NES without epilepsy). The medication tables in the *Workbook* list major CNS active medications, including AEDs used for epileptic seizures and for migraine prevention, mood stabilizers for bipolar disorder, antidepressants for depression, and anxiolytics for anxiety, providing patients with basic information about each drug. The medication and side effect list is not exhaustive, and new medications are being released every year.

The *Workbook* encourages patients to write down any questions or observations to discuss with you and their prescribing physician about their CNS active medications and create a medication list.

Why Is It That Some Medications Have to Be Taken Three Times a Day, and Others Are Only Given Once a Day?

How often a patient takes a particular drug is determined by a laboratory measurement: the actual length of time that the specific drug remains active and effective in the body. Drugs are metabolized (broken down) by the liver and are eliminated from the body by the kidneys at different speeds. When a drug is eliminated quickly, it is said to have a short half-life—defined as the time it takes to eliminate half of the ingested quantity of the drug from the body. When a drug is metabolized and eliminated slowly, it has a long half-life.

It therefore follows that if a medication has a short half-life, it has to be taken several times during the day to maintain a steady and effective blood level. But if it has a long half-life, it can be taken once a day because the drug will remain in the body and continue to be active for a full 24-hour period. Phenobarbital has a long half-life (96 hours), and that explains why the entire day's dose can be taken at bedtime. Carbamazepine (Tegretol) has a shorter half-life (12 hours), which means that, in order to maintain a steady blood level, the day's dose has to be divided into 2 or 3 parts, to be taken every 8–12 hours.

How Does a Patient Know If He or She Is Experiencing a Drug Allergy?

An allergy to many drugs first shows up as a skin rash that may look like measles and/or raised red itchy blotches called hives. If an allergy is going to develop, it usually occurs within several days to one month from starting a new drug. If the patient develops any unexplained rash within the first month of taking a new medication, she should notify her physician immediately. The physician will investigate the rash, and if an allergy is suspected, the drug will be stopped.

Why Do Physicians Order Blood Tests for Their Patients Taking Some Anticonvulsant Drugs?

Blood levels tell the physician whether the dosage prescribed is giving an effective amount of some anticonvulsant drugs. Blood level tests are necessary because of the fact that each person responds to a given drug differently. It is necessary for the patient's doctor to measure blood levels of the patient's medicines in order to fine-tune the amount of drug the patient is taking to minimize side effects and to be sure that he is receiving an effective dose.

Why Does the Patient's Doctor Order Other Kinds of Blood Tests—Such as a Complete Blood Count or a Liver Enzyme Test?

The best way a patient's doctor can ensure that the patient is not damaging her liver or bone marrow with anticonvulsant drugs is by ordering blood tests, which measure the health of any affected organs on a regular basis. Most of the anticonvulsant drugs are capable of becoming toxic (poisonous) to one or more body organs in a small number of people, particularly if dosages are high for a long period of time.

If a drug is known to cause a decreased blood count or liver problems in a small percentage of people using it, blood tests are obtained regularly for the first 6 to 12 months after the patient starts the drug. Blood tests can then be checked one to three times per year if no problem has developed.

Although most people do not relish the prospect of going to the lab for yet another test, these blood tests are important insurance both for the patient and physician. Each time the patient gets a good lab result, she can be assured that her anticonvulsant drug therapy is in a safe range.

The following lab tests are often ordered for people on anticonvulsant drug therapy (definitions can be found in the *Workbook*): CBC (complete blood count), platelet count, SGOT (AST) or other liver function studies, and urinalysis.

What Should Patients Do if They Believe That They Are Experiencing Drug Side Effects?

It is the patient's responsibility to notice side effects such as drowsiness, fatigue, imbalance, memory problems, or sharp mood swings and to inform his physician. More serious side effects may mean either that the patient is on too high a dose or that he does not respond well to that particular drug.

How Does the Patient's Doctor Know Whether Side Effects Indicate That a Drug Dosage Is Too High?

Blood levels are a reliable way of checking on a patient's dosage. There is a **therapeutic range** (different for each AED) that indicates that the patient is receiving an effective dosage. Some individuals have seizures that can be controlled at the lowest dose, while others need to be in the higher range in order to obtain seizure control. Some people have seizures that are not controllable with a particular medication, even at a higher therapeutic dose; these individuals may develop unpleasant side effects when the dosage of medication is increased further. A few people will develop side effects even when the blood level of medication is in a mid-therapeutic range.

Why Is Anticonvulsant Drug Therapy So Complicated? Why Can There Not Just Be One Right Dose, Like There Is for Antibiotics?

Anticonvulsant medication effects and metabolism is **specific for each person.** This makes anticonvulsants very different from antibiotic medications because antibiotics have pretty much the same effect on people of more or less equal body weight.

Anticonvulsants affect each person differently. For people with epilepsy, each person's brain has a different epileptic seizure focus and responds individually to drugs. Conversely, patients with NES do not have a "seizure focus" and have medication needs that may be different from other people with similar appearing seizure disorders.

Why Are Medication Decisions Based on Trial and Error? Shouldn't It Be More Scientific?

Because the response to anticonvulsant medication is specific to each person, trial and error is often required to determine the best drug therapy program for the patient. Generally, a prescribing physician will start a low dose of one medication and will gradually increase the dosage, if necessary, until seizure control is achieved.

Many neurologists believe it is best to use only one drug at a time. Yet some people have seizures that are not controlled at a tolerable dosage of one drug. For these people it is more effective to use lower doses of two drugs together for refractory epileptic seizures. When a second medication is added, it may also require gradual dose adjustments over time, depending on response. During the period that the patient's physician is working on finding the optimum medication program, he or she may check blood levels of medicines more frequently than usual in order to find the dosage that is most effective.

What If Numerous Drug Combinations Are Tried But the Patient's Seizures Do Not Stop?

About 20–30% of people with epileptic seizures (more than 50% of those with complex partial epileptic seizures) continue to have seizures on optimum drug therapy, even after thorough trials on different combinations. Some of these people may have experienced total seizure control on medications, only to develop severe side effects or to show evidence of toxicity that required the medication to be stopped or decreased. Others continue to have some seizures no matter what drugs they take because they have a kind of seizure that just cannot be fully controlled with drugs.

In all of these situations, a ***primary emphasis in using anticonvulsant medicines should be placed on the quality of an individual's life***, not only on the person's number of seizures. Sometimes it is better to tolerate a few seizures than to have the intolerable side effects that can occur on the higher prescribed doses of medicine to obtain total control of seizures.

Like any medical treatment, the benefits of anticonvulsant drug therapy have to be weighed against the risks and negative effects of the therapy in each individual case. Remember that the goal is to improve the overall quality of a person's life, and to decrease the deleterious effects that having a seizure disorder has on that person's health and well-being.

CASE VIGNETTE SUMMARY

A. T. had complex partial epileptic seizures for 15 years. After trials on a variety of different medicines, it was found that A. T.'s seizures were controlled best with carbamazepine. But A. T. told his doctor that the medicine caused memory problems, severe enough that he sometimes lost track of what he was doing. When his doctor tried him on phenytoin and then valproate, his memory improved but he had more frequent seizures. He was frustrated because while he had fewer seizures on carbamazepine, he could not remember things and his life was more impaired. A. T. and his doctor made the decision to use valproate and tolerate more seizures because it was the best alternative in terms of his overall ability to function, to think, and to live his life fully.

Complex Partial (Focal Dyscognitive) Epileptic Seizures and Medications

Since total control of complex partial epileptic seizures is so elusive, it is particularly important that individuals with this form of seizures learn other ways to reduce seizure frequency and severity and to cope with effects of their seizures. A majority of these individuals also experience generalized tonic-clonic epileptic seizures that are more effectively controlled with medications. Therefore, it is especially important to balance positive and negative effects of medications in these individuals so that they can participate fully in Sessions 4 through the end of this *Workbook*.

CASE VIGNETTE SUMMARY (modified for NES)

S. G. has complex partial seizures 4–5 times per week, and at times of stress up to 4–5 times per day. Use of carbamazepine 300 mg three times daily resulted in an initial reduction of seizures to 2–3 per week with a therapeutic blood level of 7 mcg/ml (therapeutic range 3–10 mcg/ml). Seizures persisted on numerous AED trials, and a video EEG revealed NES. Because AEDs do not treat NES, and S. G. had problems concentrating, reading, and remembering things. S. G. and her physician decided to taper off carbamazepine and to continue working from Session 4 to the end of the Workbook.

Additional Information on Anticonvulsant Medication

If you are interested in learning more about anticonvulsant medication, refer to the *Workbook*, which covers a number of additional topics, including the following:

- The impact of anticonvulsant medication on nutrition and pregnancy,
- The use of alcohol and drugs with anticonvulsant medication,
- Drug interactions,
- Forgetting to take anticonvulsant medication, and
- Driving while taking anticonvulsant medication.

You will be assisting the patient to make a joint decision with his or her prescribing physician about current drug therapy (i.e., does it/do they need to be increased, decreased, discontinued or left unchanged?). The educated patient is better equipped to make the informed decision about his medications. This is part of self-management.

Read the session goal from the Workbook *aloud with the patient.*

Goal

The goal of this session is for the patient to make a joint decision with his or her prescribing physician and with you about potential medication changes (increased, decreased, or discontinued) before or while proceeding with the rest of the sessions. Realize that the change decided upon may be implemented over time, e.g. tapering or titration of medications, as the rest of the sessions are completed.

Obstacles

There can be many obstacles in the way of the patient's ability to discuss medication with the prescribing physician. You can assist the patient in identifying possible obstacles.

Review the obstacles that the patient selected in the *Workbook* and discuss these. The full list of potential obstacles can be found in the *Workbook*, and the list below highlights some of the more common obstacles faced by patients:

- Lack of understanding about the benefits of anticonvulsant drug therapy.
- Lack of understanding of the possible side effects of drug therapy—and how to work with the physician to deal with them.
- Lack of communication between the patient and physician about medications, for example: "When I didn't like feeling so sleepy on my medicines, I just stopped taking them."

Tools

Tool #1: The Written Explanation About Central Nervous System Active Medicines Given in the Patient *Workbook* Chapter

The purpose of this tool is to provide patients with the basic information needed to be informed participants in their drug therapy program.

Tool #2: Communication Among the Patient, the Prescribing Physician, and You About the Patient's Medicines

Improving communication with the physician and seizure counselor about medicines is essential for establishing the best drug therapy program for the patient, as well as enabling the patient to become an active partner in decisions about his or her drug therapy program. An active partner is well-informed and participates in the decision-making process, especially when trade-offs are involved, such as tolerating more small seizures to minimize side effects or, alternatively, having fewer seizures but feeling slightly off-balance or drowsy.

Review Patient's In-Office Discussion Work

Review the patient's in-office discussion paperwork regarding questions and concerns about anticonvulsant drug therapy. This information will be used by the patient if the patient's prescribing doctor calls in to your appointment (or when she meets with her prescribing physician separately) to make an informed decision about tapering AEDs in lone NES if appropriate.

Review of Completed Assignments

When reviewing the patient's in-office discussion work, review the patient's completed homework assignments.

1. Seizure Log
2. Journal-keeping

3. Goal-Setting

4. "Session 3: Deciding About Your Drug Therapy" reading

5. Inquire if the patient contacted his prescribing physician to let the doctor know the patient would be discussing his medications with you and making important decisions regarding these medications. Have the discussion with the patient, even if the prescribing physician cannot participate in the appointment to equip the patient for the discussion.

6. Review the Obstacles to Session 3.

7. At the end of the appointment discussing Session 3, assign the next session, "Learning to Observe Your Triggers," to be completed by the patient prior to the next appointment.

Challenging or Problematic Responses

Session 3 contains a wealth of medication information that most patients will not have been exposed to prior to this treatment. At times the patient might feel overwhelmed by the reading material. It is important to acknowledge that this is a lot of new information to absorb; however, the patient should be encouraged to reread the chapter until she feels like she has assimilated the content. Rather than:

- P: "I can't comprehend it the first time. I have to go back and reread it."
- SC: "Some of the material may be difficult to understand the first time."

Consider: "You may need to reread things a couple of times. To learn material, it takes work to retrain your brain from old patterns and to learn new habits and approaches."

This therapy incorporates empathy and validation, while going a step further, with challenging the recurrent complaint/thought/limitation/protestation with establishing healthy boundaries with others, limit setting, and pushing one step further, as tolerated. Rather than:

- SC: "What other questions do you have about the session?"
- P: "I didn't think the medication list was appropriate."

SC: "That's fine. There's a lot of material in here that's reading material to inform patients about their medications. There are some questions toward the back."

Clinically, if a patient devalues a section he deems unimportant, he may do so with other challenging sections in subsequent sessions, and may generalize that behavior to relationships, tasks, and so on.

Consider instead: "The reading material is there to educate you to make an informed decision about your medication with your prescribing doctors. Make sure to read all of it and interact with the *Workbook* material as best you can. If you have difficulty completing the assignment, feel free to bring your questions/challenges into the appointment, after you've given it your best shot."

The therapist is not taking on a pedantic role, but rather is trying to help the patient comprehend once the patient has attempted to gain an understanding of the concepts and material.

CHAPTER 6

Session 4: Learning to Observe Your Triggers

(Corresponds to *Workbook* Chapter 5)

MATERIALS NEEDED/TASKS

- Seizure Log
- Journal
- Goal-setting
- Medication Log/questions
- Thought Record (TRs continue throughout; patient should have extra copies of the blank template)
- Patient's completed Session 4, "Learning to Observe Your Triggers"
- Session 5, "Channeling Negative Emotions Into Productive Outlets," to assign at end of appointment

APPOINTMENT OUTLINE

- Review homework assigned in the previous session.
- Identify obstacles the patient might have about accomplishing goal of recognizing triggers.
- Review reading exercises.
- Discuss completed self-observation exercise.
- Discuss completed Trigger Chart.
- Review accomplishment of (or barrier to) a small, realistic, action-oriented goal.
- Complete a Thought Record with patient at end of appointment.
- Assign homework, Session 5.

- **Goal:** The goal of Session 4 is to teach the patient how to recognize NES "triggers" (i.e., the physical, external, or internal factors and events that lead to negative states and often result in seizure episodes). This is achieved by emphasizing the interrelationships among environment, cognition, mood, physical sensations, and behavior. By learning to recognize seizure triggers, the patient will become skilled at modifying triggers when possible as a means of reducing seizure frequency.

- **Obstacle:** Ask the patient to discuss what she identified as potential obstacles to trigger identification, including the common belief that seizures "just happen," an unwillingness to take any responsibility for triggers ("I can't help the way I feel"), or finding self-observation to be too challenging.

- **Assignments:** Instruct the patient to continue with the Seizure Log and journal, as well as to complete a trigger identification strategy chosen from a goal list (e.g., write down potential triggers following a seizure episode).

- **Tools:** In preparation for the appointment, the patient was instructed to have completed a self-observation exercise as a strategy for learning how to identify physical sensations, emotions, and thoughts. At the end of the appointment, you will do a Thought Record with the patient.

Therapist Behaviors

The goal of Session 4 is to teach the patient how to recognize seizure triggers. Learning how to identify seizure triggers is a potent tool for the patient who is learning how to take control of her life because trigger identification will enable to the patient to avoid or modify some triggers, thereby reducing the frequency of her seizures. It is probable that until reading this session, the patient never believed that trigger identification was possible for her NES.

The interrelationships among environment, cognition, mood, physical sensations, and behavior are introduced as a powerful model for trigger identification. The patient is taught that there is a strong correlation between environmental stressors/external triggers (e.g., fighting with spouse), negative mood or somatic states (e.g., anger/fatigue), and target symptoms (NES). By solidifying these psychosocial relationships, the patient will learn that a wide variety of factors can impact the brain and body and aggravate the tendency to have seizures.

How Do Triggers Lead to Seizures?

As the patient reads and observes more about triggers, he will learn that his NES are precipitated and influenced by a variety of factors. In the *Workbook*, the term "trigger" is used to describe stressful circumstances, which might be an external event, such as an argument or a poor night's sleep, or an internal event, such as a feeling of anxiety.

Triggers do not always lead to symptoms, but they do lead to a feeling of "dis-ease" (i.e., a sense of disharmony of body, emotion, or thought). In the patient *Workbook*, the sense of dis-ease is described as a "negative state." A trigger brings about a negative state, which may lead to the target symptom (see Table 6.1).

Table 6.1 Examples of Trigger, Negative State, Target Symptom Pattern

Examples:

TRIGGER	⟶	NEGATIVE STATE	⟶	TARGET SYMPTOM
Triggers		Negative States		Target Symptoms
Not enough sleep	→	Fatigue, irritability	→	Headache
Criticism from parent or spouse	→	Feelings of inadequacy and anger	→	Seizure
Worry about a job interview	→	Fear of failure	→	Insomnia

This pattern is a critical discussion for you to have with the patient, given that it introduces the idea that seizures can be precipitated by environmental stressors and negative mood states, rather than something medical. Although everyone experiences similar environmental stressors and negative mood states on occasion, we all respond differently to them, and for some people the result can be NES. You can explain that *triggers* are simply the factors in a person's life that lead to *negative states*, emotions, thoughts, and sensations, which in turn produce *symptoms*. Although these negative states and symptoms are unpleasant, it is the body's way of telling the person that he needs to manage his life differently in order to achieve health and well-being. *Walk through Table 6.1 (which is Figure 5.2 in the* Workbook *) with the patient, showing a couple of examples leading to target symptoms of headache and seizure.*

Helping Patients to Recognize Their Triggers

Triggers of seizures and other target symptoms can be categorized as physical, external and internal:

- **Physical triggers** are physical factors that affect the body and brain in such a way as to increase the tendency to have seizures. Some common examples include missed medications, drug or alcohol abuse, and illness itself. Physical triggers also include stimuli such as light, sound, touch, or movement, which produce seizures in people with specific reflex epileptic seizures and in some with NES.
- **External triggers** are outside factors or events that lead to negative feelings and thoughts, which in turn may lead to seizures. Examples include difficult interactions such as arguments and rejections, and anxiety-producing situations such as job demands or school pressure.
- **Internal triggers** are moods/emotions that are self-generated (e.g., sadness, anger, or inadequacy). Sometimes the feeling starts as a direct response to a person or event (an external trigger) but continues or recurs long after the situation that triggered it is over (e.g., ruminating over a past conflict/insult). At other times, a bad feeling

will occur spontaneously without any apparent cause. Internal triggers are usually the most difficult triggers to identify because people tend to ignore or fight these uncomfortable feelings to try to make themselves feel better. As the patient begins to observe these triggers, she should remind herself that knowing her true feelings, rather than denying them, will help her to become more accepting of herself and more in control of seizures.

Common Triggers to Seizures

(Some examples from the Workbook *are listed below.)*

Physical Triggers

Lack of sleep

Illness

Injury

Pain

Specific light, sound, or touch stimuli

External Triggers

Criticism

Arguments

Loss or threatened loss of relationship

Loss or threatened loss of job

Death of a loved one

Pressure from school, job, marriage, financial problems, and so on

Overwork (job, home, school, etc.)

Internal Triggers

Anger

Fear

Anxiety

Boredom

Review the exercise to assist the patient in identifying trigger(s).

Read the session goal from the Workbook *aloud with the patient.*

Goal

The goals of this session are (1) for the patient to recognize his or her "triggers" (the physical, external, or internal factors and events that lead to negative states and often result in the target symptoms of seizures); and (2) to learn to modify triggers, when possible, as a means of reducing seizure frequency.

Obstacles

There can be several obstacles to trigger identification. You will be assisting the patient to identify possible obstacles.

Review the obstacles that the patient selected in the *Workbook* and discuss these. The full list of potential obstacles can be found in the *Workbook*. The list below highlights several of the more common obstacles faced by patients:

- Most people are unaware of this process. They may view their seizures as purely random or as happening for "no good reason."
- Patients often feel frustrated, angry, or depressed about trying to identify their triggers. They may blame themselves and feel like failures if they cannot observe their triggers immediately.

Blame and Guilt: A Cautionary Note

The second obstacle above refers to a particularly important obstacle that warrants further discussion. When a patient is informed that he has some ability to take control of a problem such as NES, there is a tendency for the patient to blame himself (e.g., "It's all my fault I have seizures;

I should have been able to get control of this before"). Additionally, a patient might feel guilty for not adhering to all the guidelines used in this program, which can lead to self-reproach (e.g. self-talk, "I didn't do *all* the homework—no wonder I'm such a failure!").

> ✓ **Clinician's Note**
>
> *Emphasize to the patient that no one can follow* all *of the suggestions of this program* all *the time, and that* not *completing everything does not mean the patient is a "failure." This program offers people an opportunity to gain more control over the troublesome symptom of seizures. No one is expected to do this quickly or easily. Nor can everyone expect to get the same results because each person is working with a unique personality, a different brain, and his or her own individual set of life circumstances.*

Slacking Off: What to Do Instead of Feeling Guilty

On the other hand, people certainly do slack off in programs such as this one, where the status quo is challenged. They might stop reading and completing assignments at home. They cease self-observation, or they start skipping appointments. Sometimes they know why they do this, and sometimes they do not. Your role is to encourage these patients to review the material from Session 1, including the initial decision to "take control." You can refer the patient to read what she wrote in the column for motivating factors to remind her why she signed up for the program as a way to encourage her to stay the course. Additionally, obstacles to taking control should be addressed at this time.

> ## CASE VIGNETTE SUMMARIES
>
> *L. B. had complex partial seizures starting at age 12. In his early twenties, his seizures became less frequent. At the age of 25, his seizures consisted of twitching of the left arm and face, with stiffening of his left leg—sometimes causing him to fall. L. B. lived with his parents and he wanted very much to please his father, who expected a lot from him and would often tell L. B. that he could get better grades. During office visits, L. B.'s left arm and face would begin to twitch slightly when discussing his father.*

During a self-observation practice exercise, his counselor asked him to think about his father and observe the feelings that resulted. L. B. thought about a recent conversation he and his father had had. He was able to observe that he felt inadequate to meet his father's expectations—and very much afraid of failure. L. B. noticed that conversations with his father frequently triggered his seizures. He observed that even thinking about his father was sometimes a trigger for seizures. The negative state that resulted was one of feeling inadequate and afraid he would fail.

During subsequent appointments with his seizure counselor, L. B. worked on developing ways to avoid or reduce this particular trigger. He also learned to channel his negative state (fear of failure) into positive outlets, instead of having seizures.

———

A. W., who was in her mid-thirties and worked as a waitress, called her doctor and left a message that she was "having seizures all the time." From age 8 she had had absence seizures, which were in good control as long as she took her medication. During her teenage years she stopped taking her medicine several times and had had a flurry of seizures.

When A. W. came in to see her doctor, she told him quickly that she knew why she was having seizures again. She had a new boyfriend, and she had started taking some stimulant street drugs when they were out together. She also had been missing out on a lot of sleep. At her doctor's suggestion, she wrote down three physical triggers that in her experience brought about seizures:

"My triggers: Skipping medicine (teenage years), taking drugs, missing sleep."

A. W. decided she would try avoiding these three triggers and see if she still had seizures. As she and her doctor had hoped, her seizures promptly stopped.

Tools

Review Patient's In-Office Discussion Work

Review the patient's in-office discussion paperwork including the Tools: Self-Observation exercise and the Trigger Chart.

Review of Completed Assignments

When reviewing the patient's in-office discussion work, review the patient's completed homework assignments.

1. Seizure Log
2. Journal-keeping
3. Goal-setting
4. "Session 4: Learning to Observe Your Triggers" reading
5. Medication Questions (address any residual questions that arose)
6. Review the Obstacles to Session 4.
7. Review Tool: Self-Observation. Review the patient's self-observation exercise. Was the patient able to achieve relaxation, notice physical sensations, observe thoughts and emotions?
8. Trigger Chart: Review the patient's Trigger Chart to ensure that she is able to differentiate between physical, external, and internal triggers, as well as the negative states that the triggers create and the resulting targeted symptoms.
9. Review "Going Further" sections, and discuss a preliminary Trigger Plan.
10. Complete a Thought Record with the patient at the end of the appointment. [Make sure to allow *at least* 15 minutes at the end of the appointment to complete the Thought Record.]
11. At the end of the appointment discussing Session 4, assign the next session, "Channeling Negative Emotions Into Productive Outlets" to be completed by the patient prior to the next appointment.

Preliminary Plan for Addressing Triggers

Now that the patient has begun to identify seizure triggers, he can make a plan for addressing one or more of those triggers as a way to reduce seizure frequency. Review what the patient wrote about avoidable triggers (e.g., not enough sleep) and unavoidable triggers (e.g., having the flu). In preparation for the appointment, the *Workbook* instructed the patient to have completed a series of questions and a plan for addressing an identified trigger:

- Triggers that I can probably address
- Triggers that I probably cannot avoid
- Triggers that I may be able to modify sometimes
- I want to make a plan to address the following trigger
- This is my plan for addressing this trigger
- After trying to follow this plan, these are my observations about how it went

Review the patient's responses in the appointment.

Do a Thought Record With the Patient in the Appointment

At the end of *Workbook* Session 4, there is a Thought Record (TR) example for the patient to have examined prior to this appointment. For therapists familiar with using a TR, the following is a review emphasizing the use of the TR for patients with seizures. For therapists who have not conducted a TR, the following information is essential to help understand the importance of the TR in the process of a patient taking control of her seizures.

Prior to coming to the appointment, the patient was instructed to read the TR, but not to complete one on his own. At the end of the Session 4 appointment, you will guide the patient through a TR on the blank page in the patient's *Workbook*, asking the questions for each column and those for getting to the core thought. You will act as scribe for the *first time* the patient does a TR in the appointment. Thereafter, the patient guides himself through the TR and writes his own answers. The first time going through a TR may take 15–20 minutes, so make sure to be aware of time during the appointment to include this exercise. The TR is one of the most powerful Tools the patient will have in the process of taking control.

A blank Thought Record with columns can be printed by patients or therapists from www.MindOverMood.com or from the book *Mind Over Mood* by Dennis Greenberger and Christine A. Padesky, (©1995, The Guilford Press), which gives them permission to make copies of the form for their patients and also offers further guidance on using Thought Records with their patients. The *Clinician's Guide to Mind Over Mood* is also helpful for this purpose.

In future appointments, along with reviewing the Seizure Log and pertinent journal entries, you will review TRs that the patient has completed at the beginning of the appointments as a check-in and as a segue into session content. The first time you do a TR with the patient in the appointment, refer to the instructions in the *Workbook* for administering a TR. For the first TR, pick a recent seizure and use it to identify the situation (what happened just before the seizure).

- The first 3 columns of a Thought Record are used to distinguish a situation from the emotions and the thoughts the patient had in the situation. Have the patient provide as much detail about the situation as possible, "Like you are reading a scene in a book." List the moods at that event and rate each mood on a scale, 0 to 100. Keep the situation, moods and thoughts separate in separate columns.
- Identifying and listing Automatic Thoughts may reveal the Hot Thought (or Core Belief) that lies at the bottom of the issue or concerns. Ask questions given at bottom of Patient Example to help the patient get below the surface thoughts to what lies beneath.
- The next columns in the Thought Record lists evidence that does and does not support the Hot Thought that the patient identified and chose.
- The Alternative Thought column of the Thought Records is where a "Balanced Thought" provides an opportunity for the patient to develop new ways of thinking that can lead to feeling better. Rate how much the patient believes the Alternative Thought on a scale, 0 to 100 (100 is fully believe).
- Following the Balanced Thought, the last column is where current moods are listed and re-rated for their intensity.

- Compare the change in mood scores from what was written at the time of the event to after completing the exercise.
- Patients can see with successful use of a Thought Record that changing the way they think can change the way they feel.
- As in developing any new skill, underscore to the patient that he or she will need to practice completing many Thought Records before consistent results are achieved.
- Emphasize that the Thought Record can be used at the onset of symptoms to prevent the progression, or can be used afterward to process what may have triggered the symptoms.

Discussion on the Target in the Thought Record Used in This Therapy for Seizures

Beck writes, "The cognitive model states that the interpretation of a situation (rather than the situation itself), often expressed in automatic thoughts, influences one's subsequent emotion, behavior, and physiological response. . . . Certain events are almost universally upsetting . . . People with psychological disorders, however, often misconstrue neutral or even positive situations and thus their automatic thoughts are biased. By critically examining their thoughts and correcting thinking errors, they often feel better" (Beck, 1995, p. 75).

Ultimately, using the TR in this therapy, the therapist is trying to get to the patient's core belief(s). Our role as therapists is to guide the patient through the superficial and intermediate-level thoughts. If you perceptively identify a core belief for a patient during the formulation or tools discussion, for example the issue of inadequacy, in the approach used in this treatment, do not provide the interpretation for the patient. Rather, your role is to help the patient look back to identify the core issue for him- or herself. The process of guided self-discovery occurs working through the TR from the target symptoms (e.g., "I had a seizure on Monday").

Discussion of Conceptualizations on Cognitive Therapy: The Cognitive Model from Beck (Beck, 1990)

Core beliefs

↓

Intermediate beliefs

(rules, attitudes, assumptions)

↓

Situation → Automatic thought → Reaction

(emotion, behavior, physiological)

Core beliefs are fundamental understandings and ideas (content) regarded by a person as absolute truth—absolutistic statements about ourselves, others, or the world. Core beliefs are the deepest cognitions and often come from childhood, and while firmly believed may not necessarily be true in life. They may remain fixed if they developed from traumatic experiences or consistent life experiences.

Techniques to identify core beliefs include looking for recurring themes in a Thought Record or using the downward arrow technique.

We use the **downward arrow** technique examining situation, automatic thought, and reaction to get through intermediate beliefs (assumptions), down to *core belief* (specifically centered on "I am"). The "I am" core is often where the most revelation and transformation occurs.

Keep asking, "What does this mean about me?" to reveal a core belief, an absolute that seems unchangeable. Some of the questions to get from an Automatic Thought to the Hot Thought include, "What is the worst thing that could happen, if this were the case? What am I most afraid of, if this were true? What images or memories do I have in this situation?"

Beck notes that common **negative core beliefs** are helplessness, worthlessness, and unlovability. Beck defines **schema** as cognitive structures within the mind (the content of which are core beliefs). For the patient with characterologic traits, schemas are strongly held negative core beliefs. Padesky notes, "the maladaptive schemas of clients with lifelong problems are believed to maintain their difficulties because they are not balanced by the presence of adaptive schemas" (Padesky, 1994).

Cognitive Themes to Identify Core Beliefs

- I am
- Others are
- The world is

Intermediate thoughts (assumptions) operate as rules guiding our daily actions and expectations.

Automatic thoughts (ATs) can be in verbal form (words, phrases), visual form (images), or both.

Techniques to explore ATs include:

- Exploring spontaneous thoughts/images (T/I)
- Following T/I to completion (to the point of getting through or to an ultimate catastrophe)
- Jumping ahead in time (if following to completion leads to only more obstacles with no end in sight)
- Coping in the T/I (having the patient cope with the thought, as each problem arises)
- Changing the T/I (reimagining or changing the ending)
- Reality-testing the T/I (test with evidence for/against, or compare to what is really happening)
- Repeating the T/I (if exaggerated, noncatastrophic, outcome)
- Substituting, stopping, and distracting oneself from T/I.

Challenging or Problematic Responses

Session 4 contains a number of concepts, and it is not unusual for some patients who do not have the "psychiatric stamina" or tools to address challenging emotional issues to become overwhelmed or frustrated with the program:

- P: "To be totally honest with you, I was going to call you and say 'I give up.'"

Patients may become leery of treatment if they feel overwhelmed with the work and, as a result, they see an increase in their seizures. When patients make the statement, "I was thinking about quitting," you can refer to the common pattern, "What you are thinking is frequently experienced by patients with NES. The NES treatment research shows patients typically have a bump in their seizure counts. Why do you think that may happen?"

After the patient responds, validate or correct the answer:

"When you start to make changes in your life, sometimes your body reacts. Like when you are working out or exercising, sometimes your muscles hurt. That isn't necessarily bad. It is your body responding to being challenged physically. The seizures may be a response to your emotions being challenged. Over time, the majority of patients who had the initial rise eventually had a significant reduction in their seizures, if they stuck it out and learned the tools over time for taking control of seizures."

- P: "I was ready to throw in the towel."
- SC: "It takes practice and time."

Along with reinforcing practice, consider responding:

"Do you remember what we said in the early appointment about motivation? Let's take a look at what you wrote in Session 1 under Motivating Factors. [*Turn to the page where patient wrote his answers.*] Here is the reason that you are doing the hard work you are doing. When you signed on the line in that session, you were committing to yourself to start the process of taking control of your seizures. When you have the feeling of giving up, feel free to go back to review what your motivations were to help push through the hard times."

CHAPTER 7

Session 5: Channeling Negative Emotions Into Productive Outlets

(Corresponds to *Workbook* Chapter 6)

MATERIALS NEEDED/TASKS

- Seizure Log
- Journal
- Goal-setting
- Trigger chart
- Thought Record (TRs continue throughout; patient should have extra copies of the blank template)
- Patient's completed Session 5, "Channeling Negative Emotions Into Productive Outlets"
- Session 6, "Relaxation Training: Experiencing the Sensation of the Brain Changing Itself" to assign at end of appointment

APPOINTMENT OUTLINE

- Review homework assigned in the previous session.
- Identify obstacles the patient might have about accomplishing goal.
- Review reading exercises.
- Discuss completed Trigger Chart.
- Review any Thought Records.
- Assign homework, Session 6.

OVERVIEW

Goal: In Session 4 the patient learned how to identify "triggers" that lead to "negative states," which can produce symptoms such as seizures (e.g., criticism from a parent might lead to feelings of inadequacy and anger, which can trigger a seizure). In Session 5 the patient learns how to channel negative states into productive outlets that help prevent seizures or other target symptoms (e.g., headaches). This is achieved by helping the patient learn to honestly "express" thoughts and feelings, to practice "self-acceptance" (e.g., a compassionate attitude toward oneself), to view negative states as a "demand for action," and finally, to "take action" by addressing the cause of a negative state directly (e.g., telling critical parents that you will not have dinner with them unless they agree not to be critical) or by reducing the effects of a negative state through other channels (e.g., exercise, vigorous work, hobbies).

- **Obstacle:** Ask the patient to identify potential obstacles to taking positive action in response to a negative state, including externalizing blame, and blaming self or other circumstances for a negative state.
- **Assignments:** Instruct the patient to continue with the Seizure Log and journal, create a goal list and how to take positive actions to achieve listed goals, practice a relaxation exercise, and complete any Thought Records.
- **Tools:** In preparation for the appointment, the patient was instructed to practice channeling negative states into productive outlets using strategies discussed in the reading materials, including expression, self-acceptance, viewing negative states as a demand for action, and taking positive action.

Therapist Behaviors

In Session 4 the patient learned how to identify "triggers" that lead to "negative states," which can produce seizures. In Session 5 the patient learns how to channel negative states into productive outlets. Specifically, the patient learns how to prevent seizures by addressing identified triggers for seizures, either directly or indirectly. The patient achieves this skill through self-expression, self-acceptance, viewing the negative state as a demand for action, and by taking action.

Figure 7.1 illustrates the basic tasks of Sessions 4 and 5 in the *Workbook*.

```
┌─────────────────────────────────────────────────────────────────────────────┐
│  Trigger    ----//---->    Negative State    ----//---->    Target Symptom (e.g., seizure)  │
│                                                                             │
│              Session 4                        Session 5                      │
│                                                                             │
│  Block negative state by addressing      Block target symptom, e.g. seizure, by channeling   │
│  and/or accepting trigger                negative state into productive outlets              │
│                                                                             │
└─────────────────────────────────────────────────────────────────────────────┘
```

Figure 7.1

Trigger, Negative State, Target Symptom Pattern

Productive Outlets for Negative States

The following four guidelines will help the patient to channel identified negative mood states into productive outlets:

1. *Expression*
2. *Self-acceptance,*
3. *Viewing negative mood states as a demand for action*
4. *Taking action.*

Expression

"Expression" refers to expressing thoughts and feelings honestly. Our primary moods/emotions are mad, sad, glad, jealous, anxious, afraid, and ashamed. Instruct your patients to express identified negative thoughts clearly and to acknowledge negative fears or judgments of themselves.

Self-Acceptance

Self-acceptance means seeing oneself as a worthy person, deserving of understanding, forgiveness, and respect. People with chronic illness often feel "worthless" due to the limitations imposed by the illness. Supportive relationships and counseling can help foster self-acceptance.

For many in our society, what we do defines us. You should emphasize: *your worth is not tied to what you do.*

For some patients, supportive relationships with others and professional counseling may be needed to help develop a sense that their baggage or negative qualities are OK and worthy of self-acceptance. Encourage the patient to practice self-acceptance, which can be a long process.

See Negative States as a Demand for Action

Emphasize that a negative mood state, which can occur on four levels of human experience (i.e., physical, emotional, intellectual, and spiritual), indicates a "demand for action" (e.g., feeling uneasy about accepting a dinner invitation from critical parents signals the person that she needs to make changes).

Take Action

There are two categories of "action" that people have found to be productive outlets for negative states:

1. Action aimed at relieving the *source* of the negative state

and

2. Action aimed at relieving oneself of the *effects* of the negative state.

Actions Aimed at Relieving the Source of the Negative State

Emphasize that there are a wide variety of actions that the patient might choose to take in order to relieve the source of a negative state, including the following:

- Avoiding a stressful situation, or
- Communicating one's needs clearly in an attempt to change a stressful situation by expressing clearly how a person's actions or words make the patient feel.

Sometimes it may be necessary for the patient to set limits with other people by letting them know what the patient is willing and unwilling to accept from them, in order to continue the relationship on a positive basis.

> ### CASE VIGNETTE SUMMARY
>
> *F. is a woman who finds herself feeling "negative" about a dinner invitation from her parents due to their tendency to criticize her, particularly about the fact that she has not yet found a good full-time job. With some introspection she concludes that her emotional survival is indeed threatened by the prospect of her parents' criticism and she is afraid that her parents' disapproval will only add to her own inner sense of failure. F. observes that she is also feeling angry with her parents due to their lack of support and discouragement.*

There are many actions that F. can take to address her fear and anger about having dinner with her parents (the full list is included in the *Workbook*).

1. She can tell her parents that she is too busy to accept their dinner invitation.
2. She can tell her parents that she would like to accept their dinner invitation, but only with the understanding that her job situation will not be a topic of conversation during the evening.

Action Aimed at Relieving Oneself of the Effects of a Negative State

> ### CASE VIGNETTE SUMMARY
>
> *Suppose that F. is 21 years old and is currently living with her parents. She has told her parents repeatedly over the past year that she strongly dislikes their negative, judgmental comments about her. She would very much like to live independently, but her low income from part-time employment will not allow her to move out. She avoids frequent contact with her parents, particularly mealtimes, which she often shares with friends. Today, she has decided not to avoid the dinner because she simply needs a nutritious meal and cannot afford to repeatedly eat out.*

Given that her parents are unwilling to change and she is unable to move out at this time, there are other actions F. can take to reduce her negative state (see *Workbook* for the full list).

1. Telephone a close friend to talk.
2. Take a brisk 3-mile walk.

Use the full list in the *Workbook* to demonstrate actions that people find helpful for relieving negative states:

1. Physical exercise, as in examples 2 and 9 (in *Workbook*).
2. Obtaining social support, as in examples 1 and 7.
3. Self-expression and/or talking about your worries, as in 1 and 5.
4. Vigorous activity, especially when it gives a sense of accomplishment, such as in 4 and 8.
5. Active relaxation (i.e., activities such as hobbies that are relaxing for a particular person), as in 3 and 10.
6. Escape into recreation, as in 6, 7, and the book or magazine in 10.

Putting It All Together: A Summary

Figure 7.2 (Figure 6.3 in the *Workbook*) summarizes the process described in Sessions 4 and 5.

Negative States and Target Symptoms

Review the exercise to assist the patient in developing ways to take negative states and turn them into productive outlets to prevent progression to target symptoms.

Read the session goal from the Workbook *aloud with the patient.*

Goal

The goals of this session are (1) to learn to take positive action in response to negative states, and (2) to channel negative states into productive outlets instead of target symptoms.

```
┌─────────────────────────────────────────────────────────────────────┐
│                                                                       │
│  Trigger ---//---> Strong Negative States ---//---> Target Symptom (seizures)  │
│                                                                       │
│  Block here (Session 4)      Block here (Session 5) with:            │
│                                                                       │
│                              1. Self-expression                      │
│                                                                       │
│                              2. Self-acceptance                      │
│                                                                       │
│                              3. Seeing negative state as a demand for action  │
│                                                                       │
│                              4. Taking action                        │
│                                                                       │
│                                  A:  action that relieves the source of the negative state, or  │
│                                                                       │
│                                  B:  action that relieves the negative state itself  │
│                                                                       │
└─────────────────────────────────────────────────────────────────────┘
```

Figure 7.2

Tools to Block Progression of Negative State to Target Symptom

Obstacles

The patient was asked to identify potential obstacles to taking positive action in response to a negative state. Review the obstacles that the patient selected from the list and discuss.

Examples include:

- Feeling powerless and helpless ("There's no way I can help myself out of my negative states.")
- Blaming oneself for negative states.

(These examples are frequently selected by patients with NES and are recurrent themes, which can be discussed in the appointment.)

Tools

The patient was instructed to practice channeling negative states into productive outlets through (1) expression, (2) self-acceptance, (3) viewing the negative state as a demand for action, and (4) taking positive action and encouraged to practice this skill.

Review Patient's In-Office Discussion Work

Review the patient's in-office discussion paperwork regarding channeling negative states into productive outlets.

Review of Completed Assignments

When reviewing the patient's in-office discussion work, review the patient's completed homework assignments.

1. Seizure Log (briefly review seizure counts, asking if the patient notices any new patterns)
2. Review Thought Record(s) patient may have completed to assess mastery of the new Tool. (Going forward, transition from the seizure log to using the TR for the check-in at the beginning of the appointment to help the patient process triggers and stressors when they have seizures).
3. Journal-keeping
4. Goal-setting
5. "Session 5: Channeling Negative Emotions Into Productive Outlets" reading
6. Trigger Chart and Avoiding Triggers
7. Review of Obstacles to Session 5
8. Review the patient's answers to the questions asked in the patient workbook.
9. At the end of the appointment discussing Session 5, assign the next session, "Relaxation Training," to be completed by the patient prior to the next appointment.

Challenging or Problematic Responses

Patient and seizure counselor are reviewing progress:

■ P: "I'm halfway through, and I'm doing lousy."

When a patient presents this type of discouragement, seize the opportunity to encourage and educate the patient. Patients can be overwhelmed by the many stressors in their lives and may generalize one problematic area to the condition, which may lead to catastrophizing to all areas of their lives. By reviewing the tools and progress they have made, patients can implement what they have learned and may see improvements in one area that can be highlighted.

Consider responding with:

- SC: "We typically see an increase in NES count in patients who are working in these sessions, and that can be frustrating. It doesn't happen with everyone, but the bump in seizures you are experiencing is consistent with others who have done the treatment. The bump has been interpreted as a psychological response to the hard work you are doing. In my mind, that's not 'doing lousy,' that's doing good work. Over time, for patients who gained the skills and applied them, the seizures decreased in the majority of people who did the treatment. This could happen with you, also."

CHAPTER 8

Session 6: Relaxation Training: Experiencing the Sensation of the Brain Changing Itself

(Corresponds to *Workbook* Chapter 7)

MATERIALS NEEDED/TASKS

- Seizure Log
- Journal
- Goal-setting
- Trigger chart
- Thought Record (TRs continue throughout; patient should have extra copies of the blank template)
- Patient's completed Session 6, "Relaxation Training: Experiencing the Sensation of the Brain Changing Itself"
- Session 7, "Identifying Your Pre-Seizure Aura," to assign at end of appointment

APPOINTMENT OUTLINE

- Review any Thought Records.
- Review homework assigned in the previous session.
- Identify obstacles the patient might have about accomplishing goal.
- Review reading exercises.
- Discuss completed Trigger Chart.
- Assign homework, Session 7.

OVERVIEW

Goal: The goal of Session 6 is to teach the patient relaxation training in order to demonstrate that it is possible to experience the sensation

101

of the brain changing itself. Specifically, stress can be a trigger for seizures and, although it is not fully understood, it is likely that stress changes brain wave states that potentially cause seizures. By learning how to recognize stress, the patient can potentially prevent seizures by using relaxation techniques that may alter brain wave activity.

- **Obstacle:** Ask the patient to identify any obstacles to learning relaxation training.
- **Assignments:** Instruct the patient to continue with the Seizure Log and journal, choose a small goal, practice a relaxation exercise, and complete any thought records for seizures (or symptoms).
- **Tools:** In preparation for the appointment, the patient was asked to begin practicing guided progressive relaxation training.

Therapist Behaviors

Take the patient through a progressive relaxation exercise via the body-scan script. Some patients may decide to opt out of learning relaxation, and any concerns should be addressed. If the patient has difficulty with the exercises but shows interest in continuing with the rest of the material and appears invested, encourage continued practice.

✓ **Clinician Note**

For some patients, this will be their first introduction to relaxation techniques. It is not uncommon for a patient to report feeling anxious or to even experience a panic attack while engaging in the progressive relaxation exercise. Some individuals have been experiencing unremitting stress for so long that they have forgotten what it feels like to be relaxed. Because the state of relaxation can feel foreign, it is not unusual for him or her to report anxiety. This should be normalized, and the patient should be reminded that anxiety is harmless and will go away after a few minutes.

Relaxation Training

The goal of the relaxation training exercise for persons with seizures is to teach them to reach and sustain an awake, relaxed state. This session teaches relaxation techniques *without* requiring the use of EEG bio-feedback, in an effort *not* to create an environmental dependency for the patient. If regional muscle tension is observed during the exercise, it will be necessary to work with patients to help them relax these muscles. Sometimes verbal suggestions to "open the jaw," "relax the chin," and "let go of any tension in the forehead" will suffice. It is helpful to explain that seizures may occur in a drowsy state, which is the reason for learning to avoid it with relaxation training. If the patient is unable to reach a fully relaxed state, encourage him or her to "let go" even more, with positive suggestions that "you can do it." If your patients appear sleepy, give them a problem to solve to wake them up. You may also utilize autogenic techniques, visualization, or positive thoughts (if those were helpful, from Practice Parts 2 and 3 in Session 6).

Emphasize to your patients that the goal is to keep in the awake, relaxed state as much as possible during the exercise.

The first relaxation training appointment may be underwhelming, with few successes in producing the desired awake, relaxed state. However, this appointment allows for familiarity with the exercise and setup, and some understanding of the goals of training. At the end of the first appointment, instruct your patient to spend at least 10 minutes each day practicing relaxation techniques. Each person can practice this exercise at home by remembering and running through the script internally. The ideal approach is preferably *without* an auditory recording, so as to not become dependent on the presence of equipment to do the exercise. It is important to remind your patients that very little progress will be made with relaxation training without practicing this relaxation exercise for 10 minutes on a daily basis at home. Generally, with continued practice, most individuals are able to produce an awake, relaxed state.

✓ **Clinician Note**

A note about teaching diagphragmatic breathing: In teaching deep diaphragmatic breathing, be sure to watch patients and help them avoid shallow high chest breathing (hyperventilation). In some instances, hyperventilation can precipitate seizures. On the other hand, deep diaphragmatic breathing is an effective relaxation technique that will often help patients prevent or stop seizures.)

For many people with NES, their seizures started unexpectedly and without warning. The disquieting nature of seizures can make patients believe that they do not have control over their brains, which can make them feel out of control with both brain and body. By teaching your patients how to become aware of seizure triggers, negative states, and auras more effectively—to actually change the brain's state at the moment a patient senses that he or she is going to experience a seizure—the patient can learn how to alter brain wave activity and potentially stop a seizure before it starts. This ability to change the brain's state has been demonstrated over centuries (e.g., yogis). During this appointment, the same relaxation used in EEG biofeedback sessions will be used to alter brainwave activity *without* incorporating EEG biofeedback.

How Does Relaxation Help to Reduce Seizure Frequency?

For many individuals with seizures, working with relaxation will in fact help to reduce seizure frequency. The reasons for this improvement are not fully understood. Most likely, it is the process of learning to change and control brain wave states that helps to reduce seizure frequency and give people a sense of being in control of seizure onset.

Another explanation for the benefits of relaxation training is that it helps people learn to truly relax—both mind and body. Relaxation helps to reduce the overall arousal level of the body and brain. This means that the person who practices relaxation regularly is less susceptible to stress, less tense, and less likely to have target symptoms such as seizures.

Relaxation training may help the patients learn to alter brain wave states when they are likely to have a seizure (e.g., when a pre-seizure aura is identified). Although not all seizures can be prevented, with enough practice the patient can learn how to quickly alter brain wave activity to better manage or prevent a seizure.

Will Relaxation Training Actually Give the Patient the Sensation of the Brain Changing Itself?

Yes, relaxation training is a powerful tool for patients to use in order to "take control" of their seizures. The out-of-control feeling that seizures engender undermines self-esteem, making taking control difficult. Gaining mastery over brain wave states will give patients a strong sense of control, which will help improve self-esteem.

✓ **Clinician Note**

For a complete discussion about normal brain wave states as they appear on an EEG tracing, the EEG patterns of people with seizures, and the role biofeedback plays in relaxation training, refer the patient to Appendix I in the Workbook.

Reviewing Relaxation Training

Review the training exercises to assist the patient in learning relaxation techniques.

Read the session goal from the Workbook *aloud with the patient.*

Goal

The goal of this session is to experience the sensation of the brain changing itself, through the use of relaxation training.

Obstacles

The patient was asked to identify potential obstacles to experiencing the sensation of the brain changing itself, through the use of relaxation training. Review the obstacles that the patient selected from the list and discuss.

Examples include:

- Expecting to be able to change brain state right away, without repeated practice sessions.
- Having to be "in control" at all times and not being able to become relaxed.

Review Patient's In-Office Discussion Work

Review the patient's answers to the questions asked in the patient *Workbook*.

Review of Completed Assignments

When reviewing the patient's in-office discussion work, review the patient's completed homework assignments.

1. Seizure Log / Thought Records
2. Journal-keeping
3. Goal-setting
4. Trigger Chart and Avoiding Triggers
5. Relaxation Exercise
6. At the end of the appointment discussing Session 6, assign the next session, "Identifying Your Pre-seizure Aura," to be completed by the patient prior to the next appointment.

Challenging or Problematic Responses

Patient and seizure counselor are reviewing relaxation experiences:

- SC: "So tell me about your past experience with relaxation. . . . How did that work?"
- P: "I wanted to go to bed."

The seizure counselor responded that the goal is to experience the difference between drowsy versus awake, relaxed state. What the SC should actually have done is to continue to emphasize that relaxation is not sleep, but rather, it is keeping one's mind actively engaged.

The seizure counselor can emphasize that relaxation can be used at the end of the day and also during acute states.

As with the Thought Record, emphasize that relaxation can be used as prophylaxis/prevention and also symptomatically. Implementing relaxation at the beginning and end of each day can prevent the recurrence. Likewise, when a stressful situation arises and symptoms present, doing relaxation may stop the progression of the seizure.

———

- P: "My goal is that I don't have any more seizures."
- SC: "I want you to be seizure free. That's the whole goal."

Note: In this instance the therapist misspoke; never having any more seizures is NOT "the whole goal" of the *Workbook*. The message that you convey to patients, families, and providers is very important. In light of the message, the goal of the program is not "to be seizure free," but rather, to:

1. Gain control over seizures, and
2. Develop healthy coping strategies for life's continued stressors.

(Kids will get sick, unexpected expenses will arise, accidents will happen, family members will die, and life goes on. A reality-based appraisal of life's vicissitudes is a first step of healthy coping.) Life's stressors will continue; what *can* change is how patient's *respond* to them. Likewise, completing the program does not assure that the patient will become seizure free. While many patients who complete are seizure free, and many have a significant reduction in their seizures, some do not. Those patients still can benefit from improvements in quality of life by using healthy coping and becoming more socially active, even if they continue to have seizures.

CHAPTER 9

Session 7: Identifying Your Pre-Seizure Aura

(Corresponds to *Workbook* Chapter 8)

MATERIALS NEEDED/TASKS

- Seizure Log
- Journal
- Goal-setting
- Trigger Chart
- Thought Record (TRs continue throughout, patient should have extra copies of the blank template)
- Patient's completed Session 7, "Identifying Your Pre-Seizure Aura"
- Session 8, "Dealing With External Life Stresses," to assign at end of appointment

APPOINTMENT OUTLINE

- Review any Thought Records.
- Review homework assigned in the previous session.
- Identify obstacles the patient might have about accomplishing goal.
- Review reading exercises.
- Discuss completed Self-Observation exercise.
- Assign homework, Session 8.

OVERVIEW

- **Goal:** The goal of Session 7 is to aid the patient in learning how to identify pre-seizure auras.

- **Obstacle**: Ask the patient to identify potential obstacles to identifying pre-seizure auras.
- **Assignments**: Instruct the patient to continue with the Seizure Log and journal, choose a small goal, practice a relaxation exercise, and complete any Thought Records for seizures or symptoms.
- **Tools**: In preparation for the appointment, the patient was asked to complete a Self-Observation exercise.

Therapist Behaviors

This session educates the patient on warnings that may occur before their seizures. Some patients have readily identified their aura, while others have not. Some patients may not have auras; however, a significant number of patients with nonepileptic seizures (NES) have some form of an experience that occurs prior to their full-blown event. For patients who know their aura, discuss the warning symptoms in detail, as noted below. For those who do not know their aura, explore possibilities.

The term "pre-seizure aura" refers to a symptom or group of symptoms that precede a seizure. The aura may consist of an unusual sensation, a body movement, and/or a feeling state. Examples of common auras are visualizing lights flashing, tingling in an area of the body, an abrupt change in mood, sudden fear, an unpleasant smell, dizziness, and twitching of an extremity. Auras are experienced by people with epileptic seizures and with nonepileptic seizures.

Learning to identify an aura is an important step because it will enable the patient to utilize this pre-seizure warning to "take control." In some situations, the patient may be able to prevent the seizure itself. In other circumstances, the patient will be able to avoid injury because she is aware that a seizure is about to take place.

What Areas of the Brain Are Affected in Nonepileptic Seizures and Auras?

Neurophysiologic research reveals that no abnormal brain cell firing is present during NES. The same is true for the aura experienced before

NES. The sensations experienced during an aura with NES are just as real as those of an epileptic aura; however, *no electrical discharges are observed with an NES aura, just as no epileptiform activity is present during NES.*

> ✓ **Clinician's Note**
>
> *For a discussion regarding the role of electrical discharges and auras in epilepsy, refer to Session 7 (Chapter 8) in the patient* Workbook.

Once Auras Are Identified, What Can the Patient Do Differently That Will Help Her "Take Control"?

There are two major ways that aura recognition will help the patient "take control." One way is seizure prevention, and the second way is preventing unpleasant or unsafe effects of seizures.

Recognizing an aura will help the patient prevent seizures because the patient may be able to develop some conscious control over whether the aura will progress to a seizure. Some people report that changing their brain state (as they are learning to do with relaxation training) at the time they sense an aura seems to prevent progression to a seizure. Others notice that deep breathing or relaxing in other ways—perhaps just lying down—will prevent seizures in many instances. The Thought Record can be used when an aura is noticed to prevent progression of seizures. Still others concentrate on being aware of a trigger or negative state that preceded the aura, and they are able to use one of many methods to channel negative emotions into productive outlets, as described in Session 5.

Noticing an aura can also help the patient prevent unsafe or unpleasant effects from seizures. Unsafe seizure effects include falling, which might result in cuts, bruises, concussion or other head injury; dropping objects, which may be sharp or breakable; dangers from swimming or other sports activities; and driving. Unpleasant effects from seizures might include social embarrassment from having a seizure, urinary incontinence, and disruption of social activities. An aura may give the patient a 5–15 second warning that a seizure is about to occur—at which point the patient can sit down to avoid injury, put down any knives or sharp objects, or request assistance if in a swimming pool. Simply sitting down when an aura is identified may enable someone to have a brief seizure unnoticed, after which the patient can resume activities without any injury or undue concern from those nearby.

Pre-Seizure Aura

Review the ways in which a patient can sense warnings that occur before seizures.

Read the goal from the Workbook *aloud with the patient.*

Goal

The goal of this session is to learn how to identify your pre-seizure auras.

Examples of Auras

Over the years we have worked with many patients with nonepileptic seizures, and the following is a list of the most commonly identified pre-seizure auras:

- agitation
- a feeling of strangeness
- dizziness
- anxiety and breathlessness
- a feeling of insecurity
- a sensation of electrical energy felt throughout the body
- weakness in the legs
- depersonalization
- facial twitch
- a sinking sensation

Review Patient's In-Office Discussion Work

Review the patient's answers to the questions asked in the patient *Workbook*.

Obstacle

The patient was asked to list potential obstacles to identifying pre-seizure auras from a list provided in the *Workbook*. Review any identified obstacles.

Tool

The tool in this session, "Self-Observation," is an extension of the relaxation procedure that was done with the patient when you read the relaxation script to the patient in the previous appointment. This tool builds on the patient's use of relaxation, helping the patient to observe her body and mind during a quiet period.

Review of Completed Assignments

When reviewing the patient's in-office discussion work, review the patient's completed homework assignments.

1. Seizure Log / Thought Records
2. Journal-keeping
3. Goal-setting
4. Session 7, "Identifying Your Pre-Seizure Aura," reading
5. Trigger Chart and Avoiding Triggers
6. Relaxation exercise
7. Review of obstacles to Session 7
8. At the end of the appointment discussing Session 7, assign the next session, "Dealing With External Life Stresses," to be completed by the patient prior to the next appointment.

Patient and seizure counselor are discussing aura identification:

- P: "I've identified my aura, so I'm not sure how the self-observation would apply to me."
- SC: "So, what would you like to do? You can take the aura you have and move on, or you can do the self-observation and see if you have more."

Many patients with NES are "uncomfortable in their own skin," so the Identifying Your Aura exercise is twofold in its goals. Identifying your aura may lead to seizure prevention/cessation: First, patients who identify their aura can potentially prevent the progression of the NES with the various tools/interventions they learn. Second allowing patients to do the exercise as an assignment allows them to "slow down" and to have to face the challenge and discomfort of experiencing self without distractions. Even if a patient has already identified an aura and may not have others, self-observation is useful in this regard and may help open other areas of self-reflection and monitoring, once the self-observation exercise is completed.

Encourage the patient to do self-observation, whether or not she thinks it will "help." If she resists, don't force the issue. If she is skeptical, have her set it up as an experiment.

✓ **Clinician Note**

The sessions up to this point have provided education, awareness, and tools for the patient to take control of his or her seizures. Each tool can be used to stop or prevent the seizures. As patients have made the links among triggers, negative states, and target symptoms, and have mastered communication, Thought Record, and relaxation, they are now equipped to address external stressors and internal conflicts head-on, which are covered in the next two sessions.

CHAPTER 10

Session 8: Dealing With External Life Stresses

(Corresponds to *Workbook* Chapter 9)

MATERIALS NEEDED/TASKS

- Seizure Log
- Journal
- Goal-setting
- Trigger Chart
- Thought Record (TRs continue throughout; patient should have extra copies of the blank template)
- Patient's completed Session 8, "Dealing with External Life Stresses"
- Session 9, "Dealing with Internal Issues and Conflicts," to assign at end of appointment

APPOINTMENT OUTLINE

- Review any Thought Records.
- Review homework assigned in the previous session.
- Identify any obstacles the patient might have had about accomplishing the goal of identifying and reducing stresses.
- Review reading exercises.
- Review relaxation exercise.
- Discuss stress reduction exercise.
- Assign homework, Session 9.

OVERVIEW

- **Goal:** In Session 8, the primary goal is for the patient to begin identifying external stresses in his or her life and to make a plan to reduce and cope with stress.

- **Obstacle:** Ask the patient to identify potential obstacles to identifying and reducing external stresses, including a sense of helplessness, secondary gain, and feeling "overwhelmed by trying to make too many changes at once."
- **Assignments:** Instruct the patient to continue with the Seizure Log and journal, choose a small goal, practice a relaxation exercise, work on the stress reduction chart, and complete any Thought Records.
- **Tools:** Help the patient identify major life stresses by reviewing stresses that can be reduced now, later, or probably never; setting realistic short and long-term goals for stress reduction; acceptance of stresses that can never be changed; seeking help for stresses and inner conflicts that the patient is unable to cope with alone; and taking daily action to resolve tensions.

Therapist Behaviors

In Session 4, the patient learned how to identify seizure triggers. In Session 8, emphasize the negative impact that "external life stresses" have on seizure frequency and quality of life. For many individuals, learning to recognize and manage stress enables them to take control of their seizures. Although many people recognize that they have stress in their lives, they do not often draw the connection between stress and seizures. The main goal of Session 8 is to teach the patient how to gain awareness of the factors in his or her life that are stressful and to take responsibility for relieving those stresses that are within his or her control.

> ✓ Clinician Note
>
> *In the patient* Workbook, *a number of figures are provided to illustrate various concepts introduced in this session about the stress response. You are encouraged to review this material to familiarize yourself with the different patterns.*

Dealing With External Life Stresses

External life stresses affect seizure frequency and quality of life. A **stressor** can be defined as *any life circumstance that one finds difficult to deal with*—that is, any aspect of life that causes strain and tension, therefore affecting physical and emotional health. We are including this chapter in this *Therapist Guide* because our experience shows that while most people with seizures are aware that they are experiencing stressful situations in their lives, they are not aware that these stresses have any effect on their seizures. Learning to "deal with external life stresses" is another way to "take control" of one's seizures to become a more content and healthier person.

Dealing with external life stresses means gaining awareness of factors in one's life that are stressful to an individual—and taking responsibility for relieving those factors within one's control. Long-term efforts can have the dramatic impact of reducing seizure frequency and increasing well-being.

Are "External Life Stresses" Related to the Seizure "Triggers" Described in Session 4?

Yes, they are (but maybe not in a 1:1 fashion). In Session 4, the relationship between "triggers" and the negative mood states they create—which, in turn, elicit seizures—was discussed. Three categories of triggers were introduced: physical (e.g., lack of sleep), external (e.g., criticism), and internal (e.g., anger, fear). Identification of triggers gives patients clues about the stresses in their lives. Another Trigger Chart is provided in the patient *Workbook* for Session 8, and the patient is instructed to update it with any new triggers from the first time he or she completed it.

What Exactly Is Meant by "Stress," and How Does It Affect Health?

Any life situation that causes pressure or demands change is a source of stress. For example, life changes involving family or job may cause stress. Relationship problems and financial worries often contribute to a high level of stress. In addition, personal loss through death or divorce, as well as serious health problems, may produce tension and strain—which are the telltale signs of feeling stressed.

In his book *The Stress of Life*, stress pioneer Hans Selye, MD, described the stress reaction, which is a universal response to a threatening situation. The stress reaction results from the firing of the autonomic nervous system, which prepares the body for "fight or flight" when survival is threatened. Refer to Body and Stress Figure 9.1 in the *Workbook* for an illustration of how the body responds to a major source of stress.

✓ **Clinician Note**

At this point in the appointment, you can refer to Figure 9.1 in the Workbook, *illustrating the effects of stress on the body, and discuss the impact on different body systems and organs, asking if the patient has experienced any of these effects.*

Under normal circumstances, when one experiences a "threat," whether physical (e.g., almost having a car accident, being mugged, etc.) or psychological (e.g., a reprimand from one's boss), the autonomic nervous system reacts to the source of stress by triggering the fight or flight response. Following a period of increased arousal, there is a compensatory relaxation phase and finally a return to baseline. However, when one experiences multiple stresses (e.g., a reprimand at work, arguing with a spouse daily, financial problems, etc.) and there is no opportunity for a person to experience the compensatory relaxation phase, a chronic stress pattern is created. This kind of stress pattern leads to disease.

In the *Workbook*, the patient is asked to identify and quantify his or her stressors over the past 12 months using the Life Stress Scale (Table 9.1 in the *Workbook*) developed by Holmes and Rahe (1967).

How Do These Recent Life Events Cause Stress?

The Holmes and Rahe list of stressful events involves both inner and outer change. All of these life events require change, which is stressful for human beings. The most stressful kinds of change are those that involve relationships with the most important people in our lives. When an individual experiences relationship or any other unremitting stress, the compensatory relaxation phase and return to baseline do not occur, which leaves a person in a "chronic stress pattern."

When Someone Experiences This Much Stress, What Happens to Allow for Some Relaxation?

The chronic stress pattern described above allows no opportunity for physical or psychological relaxation. Often a very stressed person will not break this pattern until "target symptoms" become so frequent or severe that the person is ill or invalided for a period of time. Specifically, a state of complete nervous exhaustion can lead to a "nervous breakdown," a heart attack, an alcohol binge, and so on. When this occurs, the message is, "It's now OK to stay in bed and just take it easy."

How Does This Model Relate to the Concept of "Triggers" Leading to Negative States to Target Symptoms?

Target symptoms act as stress reducers because they slow people down, take them out of a stressful situation, or give them a break from regular responsibilities. Of course, target symptoms are not the best way to reduce stress because having unpleasant symptoms adds to a person's stress level in the long run. A target symptom might develop into an illness or a disability when the symptom alone is not enough to adequately relieve stress.

Why Is It That Some Triggers Seem Pretty Minor, Yet Affect the Person as if the Triggers Were Major Stresses?

Sometimes a trigger elicits a negative state because it symbolizes or reminds us of some wound—or sore point—that is a source of stress within us. For example, scoring poorly on a test would probably constitute a minor stress for just about anyone. But for some people, a low test score brings up memories from the past that make it a much more powerful trigger than it might be by itself in the present. It might cause a person to remember that one of his parents repeatedly gave him the message that "you're never going to have what it takes to succeed!" He might remember his parent saying these things or he might remember it subconsciously. If the latter is the case, he might not think about any past events but simply notice that he keeps thinking, "I failed again—I'm no good!" whenever he remembers his low test score. In this case, the actual stress might be an internal feeling of inadequacy that began in childhood—and the triggers simply bring it up to the surface and make him feel badly about it, once again. This is an example of how an external stress or trigger can bring up an internal issue, which then produces a much more powerful negative state than the trigger alone might elicit.

What Are Specific Examples of Individuals Who Experience External Stresses Leading to Target Symptoms?

A Non-Seizure Example - Low Back Pain

Refer to the example in the *Workbook* of Jennifer, whose most common target symptom is low back pain. You and the patient can review the pattern described when a series of external stresses builds up in Jennifer's life, and she becomes increasingly stressed, tense, and anxious (her negative state), until an episode of low back pain occurs and the cycle ensues. At that point, she stays home from work for a day or two, stays in bed, and allows her family to assume a lot of her responsibilities while she is laid up. This situation temporarily relieves a lot of the pressure Jennifer has been having, allowing her to break the stress pattern she was in and to experience some compensatory relaxation. Although her target symptom is certainly not pleasant or comfortable, it does have the effect of relieving an intolerable level of stress and allowing periods of physical and psychological relaxation.

How Might This Process Occur With Seizures?

For people with seizures, when stress builds up, the "target symptom" is often seizures. You can review with the patient the example in the *Workbook* of Dave, who takes his anticonvulsant drugs regularly and rarely has a seizure. However, during a period of increased job and family stress, he begins to have more frequent seizures both at home and at work. In this instance, the seizures (i.e., target symptom) enable him to get a break from his job as well as his financial and marital problems.

Clarify that you are not suggesting that people have seizures on purpose to avoid stress and responsibility—but that the body and psyche must find a way to relieve the stress, and usually a target symptom is the result. Target symptoms force a stressed individual to slow down and often temporarily reduce pressures. Target symptoms can, therefore, be viewed as "healthy" warnings that a person's stress level is too high.

If Dave in the *Workbook* example does not find ways to cope with his increasing stressors, he will eventually be unable to work. At home, his relationships with family members would begin to revolve around taking care of him after he has a seizure. It is possible that he would eventually lose his job, go on disability, and be taken care of by his family like an invalid.

Although the target symptom primarily discussed in this chapter is seizures, any target symptom can become an actual disability if stress continues to increase and the person involved is not able to cope or reduce the stress. Please refer to the patient *Workbook* for other examples of target symptoms and the state of disability that occurs after prolonged stress (e.g., low back pain can lead to disabling low back pain).

The implication of this "target symptom" discussion is that having seizures is similar to having other chronic illnesses or conditions that produce symptoms. As a result, the same stress-reducing strategies utilized to address other chronic conditions can be applied to patients struggling with seizures. In addition, patients must make a choice about whether they will allow their seizures to become a permanent disability, becoming unable to work, to drive, to live independently and fully, or whether they will learn to manage their seizures, as one would any chronic affliction, and live a full, rewarding life.

For the remainder of Session 8, the patient will be involved in the task of identifying his or her external life stresses. Help the patient do some problem-solving to reduce or modify a few of these stresses. In Session 9, the patient will learn how to identify internal sources of stress, and in Chapter 10, the patient will learn relaxation methods.

External Life Stress

Review the concept of external life stressors.

Read the goal from the Workbook *aloud with the patient.*

Goal

The goal of this session is to begin identifying external stresses in your life and to make a plan to reduce and cope with stress.

Obstacle

There can be several potential obstacles to identifying and reducing external stresses. Assist the patient in identifying possible obstacles.

Review the obstacles that the patient selected from the list and discuss.

Tool: In-Office Stress Reduction Session

In preparation for this appointment, the patient completed a **Stress Reduction Chart,** which involved identifying major life stresses (e.g., job, school, family, financial, environment, and lifestyle). The patient was instructed to break the various stresses into those that can be realistically modified **now, later,** and **probably never.** They were asked to set a few **short-** and **long-term goals.** Given that some stresses cannot be changed (e.g., chronic illness, long-term debt, divorce, etc.) the patient is encouraged to **try to accept what cannot be changed.** For major stresses and inner conflicts, the patient is encouraged to ask for help from a doctor or counselor. Finally, the patient is advised to **take daily action to reduce tensions.**

A case study in the patient *Workbook* provides an example emphasizing all of these points.

CASE STUDY SUMMARY

Thirty-eight-year-old Oscar has a history of complex partial seizures that began when he was a teen. He currently works full-time and is married with two children. Despite taking medication, he continues to have seizures. Although he was skeptical at first, he was willing to work with his seizure counselor to identify possible triggers and "target symptoms." Oscar eventually identified his busy job, financial problems, arguments with his wife, having seizures, the death of his father, and an overall lack of downtime as stresses in his life. He began to realize that the coalescence of these stressors are triggers that affect his seizures.

Oscar eventually places his stresses into three categories; stress that he could address:
- *NOW (e.g., being too busy; poor communication with spouse and children),*
- *LATER (e.g., too many job demands, financial problems), and*
- *PROBABLY NEVER (e.g., having seizures, recent death of father—will be easier to cope in 3–5 years).*

After completing his Stress Reduction Chart, Oscar was eager to tackle several goals at the same time. His seizure counselor cautioned Oscar to work on one goal at a time, because working on too many goals at once increases stress. As his first goal, he decided to talk with his boss about the need to have regular work breaks, a lunch break, and ideas that would reduce work pressures. Oscar told his seizure counselor that he has been afraid to bring up these issues with his boss because he thought he had to work harder to make up for having seizures. His counselor encouraged him by helping him practice ways to talk with his boss. He decided to have a meeting with his boss in the upcoming week.

Review Patient's In-Office Discussion Work

Review the patient's answers to the questions asked in the patient Workbook, including the Stress Reduction Chart.

Review of Completed Assignments

When reviewing the patient's in-office discussion work, review the patient's completed homework assignments.

1. Seizure Log / Thought Records
2. Journal-keeping
3. Self-observation exercise
4. Goal-setting
5. If the patient is struggling with the relaxation exercise assigned in Session 6, conduct another relaxation training exercise.
6. Review of obstacles to Session 8
7. At the end of the appointment discussing Session 8, assign the next session, "Dealing With Internal Issues and Conflicts," to be completed by the patient prior to the next appointment.

✓ **Clinician Note**

Transactional versus Transformational Therapy

This therapy is designed to be more than just another 50 minute counseling session. Joe Ehrmann (2011) describes the difference between transactional and transformational coaching. All to often, sessions also are transactional, where the therapist teaches a skill offering the patient some symptomatic relief. The therapy approach in this Therapist Guide *is intended to be a transformational therapy, where the therapist abides with the patient in these sessions on external stressors and internal conflicts, walking with him or her into the crucible of the emotional abyss, and the patient comes through with a new and healthy sense of self and meaning.*

A seizure counselor asked, "What does the therapist do when patient crises arise in appointment?"

One of our roles as a therapist is to maintain stability in the face of the patient's chaos. When a patient presents in crisis, you can triage the acuity, and life-threatening events (i.e., imminent risk of harm to self or others with intent) should be addressed/referred to emergency care, appropriately. Many times, however, what are seen as emergency crises are actually urgent or sub-acute issues needing attention but not emergency department referral.

This process is frequently extended to interpersonal issues, such as when an apparent crisis in another person's life gets "absorbed" by the patient, who takes on the responsibility for the problem/issue. That anxiety of the seeming helplessness of the situation is brought into the appointment and can be felt by the seizure counselor. The key is to appropriately assess the problem, and if not an emergency, use the particular issue in the appointment to identify recurrent patterns, prior approaches, and potential current and future responses. Identify that this is apparently a periodic process. Ask the patient what tools he or she can use to address the current stressor. Review the Stress Reduction Chart to identify the current and past stressors, and then have the patient incorporate what he or she has written down on what can be done to modify or reduce the stressor now, later, or possibly never. If the patient gives broad short-term and long-term goals to reduce the stressors, ask for concrete, realistic, attainable goals. After identifying stressors and goals, address accepting what one cannot change. This portion of the discussion is usually focused on an abuser who has died or who may never have accepted responsibility for a prior action. A discussion about how one addresses things that occurred in the past may arise.

CHAPTER 11

Session 9: Dealing With Internal Issues and Conflicts

(Corresponds to *Workbook* Chapter 10)

MATERIALS NEEDED/TASKS

- Seizure Log
- Journal
- Goal-setting
- Trigger Chart
- Thought Record (TRs continue throughout; patient should have extra copies of the blank template)
- Patient's completed Session 9, "Dealing With Internal Issues and Conflicts"
- Session 10, "Enhancing Personal Wellness," to assign at end of appointment

APPOINTMENT OUTLINE

- Review any Thought Records.
- Review homework assigned in the previous session.
- Identify any obstacles the patient might have had about accomplishing the goal of identifying internal issues and conflicts.
- Review reading exercises.
- Review relaxation exercise.
- Discuss stress-reduction exercise.
- Assign homework, Session 10.

OVERVIEW

Goal: In Session 9, the primary goal is for the patient to effectively deal with internal issues by identifying conflicts, negative feelings, and issues, and learning to take care of them by conscious choice.

- **Obstacle:** The patient identifies potential obstacles to identifying and addressing internal issues and conflicts, including not wanting to know about his or her "issues," the presence of other concerns in his or her life, a feeling of hopelessness about changing, or a judgmental attitude toward oneself and others.
- **Assignments:** Instruct the patient to decide how to proceed with internal stresses and to continue with the Seizure Log and journal, choose a small goal, practice a relaxation exercise, work on Stress Reduction Chart, and complete any Thought Records.
- **Tools:** Help the patient identify internal conflicts and issues through provided questions, and lead a discussion on how to proceed after conflicts have been identified.

Therapist Behaviors

In Session 8, we explored the subject of external life stresses and how they affect health. In Session 9, assist the patient to identify internal conflicts and issues and teach the patient how the feelings, conflicts, and issues identified affect overall health and well-being. The main goals of Session 9 are for patients to (1) learn how to gain awareness of the internal factors in their lives that are stressful and (2) take responsibility for relieving those stresses within their control by working with you or another trained counselor if patients decide to explore identified internal conflicts. This session sometimes brings up issues related to the patient's developmental history, and psychodynamic elements are utilized to address them.

> ✓ **Clinician Note**
>
> *It is not surprising that, for many people, identifying external life stresses is easier to do than looking inward at personal issues and conflicts that affect how people feel about themselves and how they relate to the world. Be sensitive about how you introduce the idea that unresolved/unconscious issues and conflicts are potentially one cause of patient seizures. Your patients might be resistant to the idea that personal issues and internal conflict interfere with their ability to derive full satisfaction from relationships and life.*

For patients who decide that they wish to continue exploring personal issues and conflicts with another trained professional, emphasize that this is a process that can occur over a period of months or years. Session 9 may merely introduce these concepts and encourage interested patients to pursue this aspect of self-awareness and self-acceptance.

The *Workbook* addresses the issue of inner conflicts by having the patient read about conflicts and do self-observation. Discuss this material in the appointment.

What Kinds of Inner Conflicts and Issues Affect Health?

Introduce the discussion that inner conflicts and issues affecting personal health often involve deep-seated thoughts and feelings about ourselves. Other issues center on the relationships we form with others. Stress that, although deep-seated thoughts can be completely unconscious, there are usually inner voices that express the inner conflicts that affect us so deeply.

Personal Conflicts and Issues

(The patient was asked to have selected any relevant statements. For the full list, refer to the *Workbook.*)

- "I act superior, but I feel inferior."
- "It's his/her fault that I'm having problems."
- "I feel at fault, guilty—and I blame other people for everything."

Issues That Center Around Relationships

Some conflicts and issues seem to center on important relationships in our lives, such as marital conflicts, family, or friendship problems. The patient was asked to select (from a list of statements) how he or she feels about the people he or she loves. For example:

- "I want you to take care of me and my needs without having to tell you what my needs are."
- "It's your fault when I don't feel okay about myself."

Chronic Feeling (Emotions) States

Another group of internal issues involves negative feeling states that a person experiences so often they can be called "chronic." Emphasize that some of these feeling states can be explored and understood, while others, such as anxiety, depression, hostility/blame, anger, fear, and shame, may require the assistance of a professional counselor.

How Do Inner Issues and Conflicts Affect Health?

Health is affected by different aspects of human experience: bodily sensation, emotion, thought, and many people include the spiritual aspect, as well. Discuss that the human mind and body interact so closely that it is often difficult to separate physical well-being from psychological well-being.

Like physical symptoms such as headaches, a sore throat, or back pain, psychological symptoms have just as much impact on health. Underscore the following critical point: If the patient's body feels fine but the patient feels constantly anxious or depressed, these feelings have just as much impact on health as a headache does. In fact, sometimes headaches or other physical symptoms such as seizures actually result from these kinds of chronic feeling states (e.g. "I'm inadequate"). For some individuals, it is impossible to take positive steps to improve a health problem, such as a seizure disorder, without dealing openly with these inner conflicts first.

In working through Session 9, patients will have the opportunity to decide how deeply they want to explore their inner issues at this time. The patient's decision will enable him or her to take the first steps toward the long-term process of dealing with inner conflicts and issues.

Clarify that it is normal initially not to be aware of one's inner issues. Even with awareness of one's inner issues, it can still be difficult to get rid of them. Emphasize that the goal is not to completely *eliminate* conflicts and negative feeling states, but rather to learn about oneself and to learn to accept and take care of the parts of ourselves that have such a profound effect on health and self-esteem.

Often people are not aware of many of the most powerful issues that affect how they feel about themselves because it feels dangerous and painful to explore these issues. However, getting to know these raw, difficult parts offers us the possibility of learning to feel more at peace with ourselves—more whole.

If your patients choose to begin this self-awareness process, they are encouraged to notice when they are particularly uncomfortable (e.g., "What am I actually feeling inside at this moment that I feel so uncomfortable, confused, or conflicted?"). The patient is instructed to observe herself when finding that she is feeling one thing but doing something else—that is, when feelings and actions conflict (e.g., nervous laughter). These moments provide clues to one's inner issues.

Emphasize that self-observation should be approached with a slow gentle attitude (e.g., one or two observations daily), and that it is essential to cultivate an attitude of acceptance toward oneself. Emphasize that the process is slow and cannot be accomplished quickly. Patients should be encouraged to take a compassionate, non-judgmental outlook toward the parts of themselves that they do observe and get to know.

The following is one example from the *Workbook* that illustrates the kind of inner dialogue that may be necessary in learning to self-observe without blame:

Self-Observation Without Blame: Example #1

- *"I'm feeling really uncomfortable; what do I notice at this moment?"*
- *"I'm saying nice words to my spouse, but I'm really feeling very angry. I know what I'm angry about, but I'm afraid to say anything or do anything about it."*
- *"I shouldn't be this way—I should just learn to say how I really feel!"*
- *"Wait a minute; I'm starting to judge myself, to tell myself that I 'should' be different. I want to go back to seeing that it's so hard for me to express my angry feelings, and to try not to judge myself for it."*

With frequent self-observation, the patient will begin to identify the inner issues that come up often. Once identified, the patient can learn to take care of the feelings and conflicts that he or she becomes aware of during this process. In this section patients are given the opportunity to begin self-monitoring, where they will write about *personal issues and conflicts; issues that center around relationships*; and *chronic negative feeling states*.

Once identified, it is important for the patient to validate these issues and get to know how these issues affect feeling states, actions, and thoughts. Emphasize that there are two ways patients can validate an inner issue and learn how it affects their psyches. They can continue self-observation when the issue arises, reminding themselves to refrain from judging and simply observe what it going on, or they can get help from their seizure counselor or other professional therapist.

Emphasize that by continuing to validate uncovered issues while observing their impact on the patient's inner and outer life, the patient is gradually making the unconscious conscious. This process may allow the patient to become conscious of issues that have remained unconscious for a lifetime or buried for years.

Emphasize that once issues and conflicts are identified, the patient can make choices that put the patient in control—rather than continuing to be controlled by the unconscious parts of him- or herself. Often, compassionate acceptance of "unacceptable" parts of oneself becomes a great source of relief.

Making the unconscious become conscious allows us to know and accept who we really are and to "take control" at a whole different level—to decide how we want to take care of the vulnerable parts of ourselves. The effect of this kind of taking control gives us the power to make positive choices, to improve relationships, to limit the effects of seizures or other symptoms, and to find meaning and enjoyment in the experience of living. If a patient notes he cannot know what is in his unconscious, you can give concrete examples highlighting that he is doing the work by making connections and identifying Hot Thoughts with the Thought Record.

Making a Decision About In-Depth Counseling

Note that the process of uncovering blind spots in the psyche is a difficult one given the layers of defenses the patient has in place to protect these vulnerable places. As a result, most people need some help from another person to learn to deal effectively with internal issues. Encourage your patients to work with you or another trained counselor. At this point in the *Workbook*, the patient is provided with four options to consider when continuing with Session 9 and is asked to select *a choice:*

1. I choose to work on this process in depth with my physician or seizure counselor. (Discuss with him or her whether he or she is licensed and trained to do this kind of counseling.)
2. I choose to work on this process in depth with another trained therapist. (Ask your physician or seizure counselor to recommend some names for referral.)
3. I prefer not to work on this process at this particular time.
4. I prefer not to work in depth on this process at this time, but would like the option of discussing any issues that come up with my seizure counselor.

Internal Issues and Conflicts

Review the basic concepts of internal issues and conflicts.

Read the session goal from the Workbook *aloud with the patient.*

Goal

The goal of this session is to effectively deal with internal issues by identifying conflicts, negative feelings, and issues, and learning to take care of them by conscious choice.

Obstacle

The patient is asked to identify potential obstacles to identifying and addressing internal issues and conflicts. (The full list of obstacles appears in the *Workbook*):

- Not wanting to know about these issues—it can be painful and difficult to explore this.
- Judgmental attitude toward yourself—the tendency to dislike or even hate the parts of yourself that you uncover in this process.
- Too many other overriding concerns in your life. (This process takes time, energy, and drive. You may not want to undertake it when you are dealing with many other demands, interests, stresses, or life changes.)

Review the obstacles that the patient selected from the list and discuss.

CASE STUDY SUMMARY

The next week Oscar had a meeting with his boss. He was prepared because of the help he had from his counselor on ways to talk with his boss. Oscar managed to get past the boss's initial anger to talk about his need for regular work breaks and a lunch break, as well as streamlining the customer service process. Oscar's work on his first external stress reduction goal was successful.

Despite this success, Oscar was discouraged about the bad feelings between him and his wife. He feared that working on Session 9 would make things worse. His seizure counselor processed Oscar's anger with her and frustration with his difficulty dealing with his marriage. His counselor recommended that he could choose to pursue issues with his marriage in more in-depth therapy during appointments separate from the "taking control" sessions, either with her or a different therapist. Because he trusted her, Oscar chose to set up therapy appointments with his seizure counselor.

After discussing his marriage, Oscar noticed that he tended to get angry and blame his wife at times when he himself felt like a failure. He also remembered that his father had blamed his mother whenever anything

---

went wrong. Now as an adult, he continued this way of trying to make himself feel better by blaming his wife. Oscar came to understand that when he blamed others, he no longer had to blame himself, so it was a kind of escape hatch for him—a way to make himself feel better.

Oscar recognized that part of his problem was that he felt bad and unworthy whenever he was not doing something productive. This explained his overworking at home and contributed to his tension and fatigue, because he never let himself relax. In turn, he was irritable with his wife.

Oscar was eventually able to establish a trusting, positive relationship with his wife. In his opinion, a lot of his success had to do with his admitting to himself that he blamed her in order to avoid blaming himself. When he could be honest about this, she acknowledged that she did the same thing. After a while, the two of them were able to talk to each other about it. They made a plan about how to talk about money issues. They started going out more and visiting friends, and this did a lot to make their relationship less strained.

Over the months that he worked on these issues, Oscar returned to Session 9 in his workbook to record his insights as follows:

Personal issues and conflicts

Feel inadequate, incompetent, something is wrong with me.

See seizures as confirming this view of myself, that I'll never be truly worthy and okay.

I overwork myself to try to compensate for feeling incompetent and unworthy.

I blame others when I feel like a failure.

Issues that center around relationships

Blaming my wife in order to avoid blaming myself, especially about lack of money.

I tend to avoid close communication, especially when something is bothering me.

> **Chronic negative feeling states**
>
> *Anxiety that I'm not good unless I earn my way by working constantly—this leads to constant chores and projects at home/overtime and no breaks at work!*
>
> *I feel exhausted and irritable a lot when I overwork myself due to this anxiety.*

Review Patient's In-Office Discussion Work

Review the patient's answers to the questions asked in the patient *Workbook*.

Obstacle

The patient was asked to identify any obstacles to identifying internal issues and conflicts.

Tool

The tool in this session is the identification of internal conflicts and issues through provided questions, followed by a discussion about how to proceed after conflicts have been identified.

Review of Completed Assignments

1. Seizure Log / Thought Records
2. Journal-keeping
1. Goal-setting: Reducing external stresses
2. Session 9, "Dealing With Internal Issues and Conflicts"
3. Trigger Chart and Avoiding Triggers
4. Relaxation training, review patient's progress.
5. Stress Reduction Chart
6. Review of Obstacles to Session 9

7. At the end of the appointment discussing Session 9, assign the next session, "Enhancing Personal Wellness," to be completed by the patient prior to the next appointment.

Challenging or Problematic Responses

Patient and seizure counselor are discussing the process of making the unconscious conscious.

- SC: (reviewing Thought Record). "What was going on right before the seizure?"
- P: "I don't know. We were having dinner."
- SC: "So what does this say about you?"
- SC: "I guess I don't want people to know I could be a weak guy?"
- SC: "So what would happen if they thought you were a weak guy?"
- P: "I don't know, I guess that I was having a seizure."
- SC: "So the hot thought is, 'I am vulnerable and I am weak.' Go ahead and write that down."

The thought "I am vulnerable" can be a core belief. Let the patient identify the Hot Thought / Core Belief. Further questioning can identify with what the core issues are associated. The automatic thoughts and the hot thought (HT) may be related to a consequence of that sense of vulnerability, which may be tied to a specific event or setting. Ask, "What images come to mind when you think about that feeling of being vulnerable?" Let the patient explore the HT. He or she may remember prior relationships, traumatic experiences, or abuse, and these images and memories can be readily identified or can be latent. Ultimately, many patients have a past trauma or experience with which they associate the core belief. Giving them the psychological and emotional room to process trauma/experience in a safe place and with the structure of the Thought Record can allow them to make the link of the past experience to the present symptoms, which has been bridged by an emotion or a thought (amygdala, prefrontal cortex, and/or hippocampus). Allowing the patient to *make* the link him- or herself will allow the patient to *break* the link from the past to the symptom presentation now occurring in a different environment and a related context.

A common example is:

- I was abused by my uncle when I was younger. (situation)
- I thought it was my fault. (thought)
- I would get mad at myself for letting it happen. (mood)
- When I am with my husband now, and we have an argument and I get upset, I get seizures. I see now that I believe it is my fault even now, but I know that my husband is not my uncle. I see that my husband and I can have a disagreement and it is not the same as being abused by my uncle.

Part of the process is the therapist being comfortable with the patient feeling uncomfortable.

Past and present

With exploring the past hurts in a safe place with the therapist, patients can come to an understanding that their childhood and what happened occurred but it is not "who you are." The past can be reframed by conveying that while their narrative may influence their future (i.e., destiny), their past is not equivalent to their present identity. Powerful change can happen with personal transformation.

CHAPTER 12

Session 10: Enhancing Personal Wellness

(Corresponds to *Workbook* Chapter 11)

MATERIALS NEEDED/TASKS

- Seizure Log
- Journal
- Goal-setting
- Trigger Chart
- Thought Record (TRs continue throughout; patient should have extra copies of the blank template)
- Patient's completed Session 10, "Enhancing Personal Wellness"
- Session 11, "Other Symptoms Associated With Seizures," to assign at end of appointment

APPOINTMENT OUTLINE

- Review any Thought Records.
- Review homework assigned in the previous session.
- Identify any obstacles the patient might have had about accomplishing the goal of achieving "wellness."
- Review reading exercises.
- Review relaxation practice.
- Discuss stress reduction methods.
- Discuss enhancing personal wellness.
- Assign homework, Session 11.

- **Goal:** In Session 10, the goal is for the patient to achieve an optimum level of wellness by reviewing past successes in coping with seizures and moving toward wellness; by identifying current goals for ongoing self-care; and by using new goals to plan their own personal wellness program.
- **Obstacle:** The patient identifies potential obstacles to wellness, such as, "I've been smoking all of my life. If I try to quit, I'm afraid I'll fail and feel worse about it," or "I take my medicines and do what my doctor tells me. If I'm not happy it's my doctor's responsibility."
- **Assignments:** Instruct the patient to continue with the Seizure Log and journal, set wellness goals, and complete any Thought Records.
- **Tools:** Help the patient review areas of life where he or she is already taking good care of him- or herself and to identify areas where positive changes could be made for the future.

Therapist Behaviors

Session 10 helps the patient transition from having an illness focus to a wellness focus. Having seizures does not exclude anyone from the possibility of being healthy and fulfilled. On the contrary, having troublesome target symptoms, such as seizures, can motivate people to make the kinds of efforts necessary to achieve a high level of wellness. For those patients who use their seizures as a motivator to take care of their bodies, emotions, minds, and spirits, they will be rewarded with a sense of health and well-being achieved through their own efforts.

Review the 10 aspects of wellness and how the patient applies them. Obstacles to wellness are reviewed, and the Planning Tool (where the patient ranked the aspects of wellness) is addressed. The schedule that the patient generated from the ranked assessment list is reviewed. Encourage the patient to make changes if the goals are unrealistic (e.g., doing everything 7 days a week).

This session is the "preparation for launch" appointment, where the patient is transitioning to discharge from the treatment program. Here you and the patient discuss and review what tools the patient has mastered and those with which he or she still has difficulty.

Address how the patient will respond if symptoms recur. What will his or her plan be?

Review the literature resources listed in end of Session 10. Many of the readings apply to current situations in the patient's life.

What Does "Enhancing Personal Wellness" Mean?

Enhancing personal wellness refers to the process of taking care of all aspects of oneself—body, feelings, mind, and spirit. Each person has an optimal level of wellness that he or she can reach, and can benefit greatly from making personal choices that enhance wellness. These choices are an important part of taking control of a chronic condition or target symptom, as well as being vital for overall health and well-being.

Wellness includes all the lifestyle choices that affect your bodily health, and extends beyond into the realm of emotion, spirit, and meaning. One way of looking at the quest for wellness is to see it as the process of connecting with yourself. Being well means that you feel connected with who you really are, with your most powerful feelings, with your deepest needs, with your own vitality and capacity for creativity and love. So much of illness and disease is a result of disconnection from yourself and other people. In contrast, wellness concerns connection with yourself and with others—it involves self-awareness, compassion, and acceptance. Ultimately, wellness involves integrating yourself as a whole, healthy person.

Obstacles to Wellness

The patient was asked to identify potential obstacles to wellness (e.g., "There are so many stresses and pressures in my life, I can't even think about taking care of myself right now," "I drink too much but I'm not an alcoholic. I could stop anytime I want to. I drink because I enjoy it," etc.). See the *Workbook* for the full list.

Review the obstacles that the patient selected from the list and discuss.

Ways to Enhance Personal Wellness

In this session, patients evaluate areas of their lives where they are already taking good care of themselves. Additionally, they will identify areas where they might choose to make positive changes. The section on tension reduction and relaxation provides the opportunity for you to emphasize the need to continue to practice communication skills and relaxation exercises that your patient was introduced to in previous sessions.

The following 10 aspects of enhancing personal wellness are reviewed in depth in the *Workbook*. We encourage you to review this list in preparation for discussing the patient's wellness plan.

1. Tension reduction and relaxation (Sessions 6 and 10)
2. Good nutrition
3. Adequate sleep and rest
4. Physical fitness
5. Avoidance of harmful habits (cigarette smoking, alcoholism, drugs)
6. Social support
7. Sexuality
8. Coping with negative emotions, stress, and internal issues (Sessions 5, 8, and 9)
9. Environmental awareness and safety
10. Meaning

CASE STUDY SUMMARY

After reading the material in Session 10, Oscar was quite sure that he wanted to work on exercise as one of his relaxation goals. Using the guidelines provided in the Assignments section, Oscar decided to take a brisk 20-minute walk at least 3 times a week. He reported that he tried to integrate daily reading breaks, but he found his mind wandering with unresolved thoughts of anger toward his wife. He just did not want to sit down and read.

At his counselor's suggestion, Oscar chose two lifestyle goals, exercise and planning constructive outlets for his feelings. He would continue with his 20 minutes of walking, 4 days a week. He chose two tension-reducing methods, hitting a punching bag that he set up in his garage and journaling. Oscar would write about imagined arguments with his wife in his journal. He used the punching bag in his garage to let off steam.

The goal of improving communication with his wife was progressing. In Session 9 he began to schedule separate in-depth therapy appointments with his seizure counselor to work on marital issues. He continued to learn how to handle his angry and negative feelings constructively.

Four years later, he was walking 5 days a week and riding his bicycle in the summer. He read for pleasure and to his kids. Oscar and his wife were able to talk about problems without being triggered into anger. He was particularly pleased that he had reached a pretty good balance between work and play—a goal that had once seemed unattainable.

Review Patient's In-Office Discussion Work

Review the patient's answers to the questions asked in the patient Workbook. *Read the session goal from the* Workbook *aloud with the patient.*

Goal

The goal for this session is to learn ways to achieve your optimum level of wellness, developing your personal wellness program.

Obstacle

Discuss whether your patient's view of obstacles to achieving wellness has changed after reading about the different ways to improve health and wellness in this session.

	Low	Moderate	High	*Rank*
1. Nutrition	_____	_____	_____	_____
1a. Weight Control	_____	_____	_____	_____
2. Sleep and Rest	_____	_____	_____	_____
3. Physical Fitness	_____	_____	_____	_____

Figure 12.1

Excerpt From Establishing Priorities Chart

Tool: Establishing Priorities

The first tool in this session is to establish priorities. After reviewing the 10 aspects of wellness, the patient was instructed to indicate on the chart in the *Workbook* whether each aspect of wellness is a low, moderate, or high priority. After deciding which of the above areas of health are low, moderate, and high priority, the patient was asked to go back over them and rank them in terms of importance to his or her health and sense of well-being. In the "Rank" column, the patient listed the highest priority as "1," the second priority as "2," then 3, 4, 5, and so on, until all the applicable areas have been ranked. Review this list with the patient. (See excerpt in Figure 12.1; for the full list, refer to the *Workbook*.)

Choosing Obtainable Goals

After establishing priorities, the patient was instructed to choose three realistic lifestyle goals and one relaxation method on his or her own to practice. Here you can assist the patient in understanding the concept of obtainable or realistic goals.

Review of Completed Assignments

When reviewing the patient's in-office discussion work, review the patient's completed homework assignments.

1. Seizure Log / Thought Records
2. Journal-keeping
3. Lifestyle Goal Selection: Discuss the goals the patient selected and ways to create a manageable schedule. (e.g., jog 3 times a week, on Monday, Wednesday, and Friday; eat breakfast every day).
4. Tension Reduction Plan: Problems may have come up for your patient in practicing relaxation exercises or performing meditation. This is your opportunity to help the patient with these skills.
5. At the end of the appointment discussing Session 10, assign the next session, "Other Symptoms Associated With Seizures," to be completed by the patient prior to the next appointment.

Challenging or Problematic Responses

SC: "Are you using the relaxation exercises every day?"

P: "Yeah, but I keep falling asleep"

SC: "That's good. It means that you are so relaxed that you can sleep."

If the patient has insomnia, relaxation exercises are a helpful tool to help with sleep induction. While they can utilize relaxation to help with sleep at night, the exercise during the day is for stress reduction. The primary use of the relaxation exercise is to maintain alertness to allay internal stress or to avert the progression of a seizure.

Trouble completing Thought Records independently

Patients should now be completing Thought Records independently. Some who are having difficulty getting to the Hot Thought may be because they are not allowing themselves to drill down to the core belief. They will instead come up with a positive phrase as they approach emotionally laden areas, with an optimistic "I would work it out." Encourage the patient to take the thought to the worst-case scenario, as difficult as that may be. They need to name and confront the feared negative emotional place to truly move beyond in to the positive.

CHAPTER 13

Session 11: Other Symptoms Associated With Seizures

(Corresponds to *Workbook* Chapter 12)

MATERIALS NEEDED/TASKS

- Seizure Log
- Journal
- Goal-setting
- Trigger Chart
- Thought Record (TRs continue throughout; patient should have extra copies of the blank template)
- Patient's completed Session 11, "Other Symptoms Associated With Seizures"
- "Taking Control: An Ongoing Process" to assign at appointment end

APPOINTMENT OUTLINE

- Review any Thought Records.
- Review homework assigned in the previous session.
- Identify any obstacles the patient might have had about accomplishing the goal of recognizing, accepting, and coping positively with the inner states and sensations, and/or behavioral and emotional symptoms associated with seizures.
- Review reading exercises.
- Review relaxation practice.
- Discuss stress reduction methods.
- Discuss enhancing personal wellness.
- Provide patient with final reading, "Taking Control: An Ongoing Process."
- Termination: Discuss patient's impressions of how they have changed, and what they have learned during the treatment.

- **Goal:** The goal of Session 11 is to help the patient recognize, accept, and cope effectively with the inner states and sensations, and/or behavioral and emotional symptoms, that constitute the "other symptoms of seizures." By normalizing these disquieting experiences as part of the seizure sequelae, the patient will feel less alone and more in control.

- **Obstacle:** The patient identifies potential obstacles to recognizing, accepting, and coping positively with inner states and sensations, and/or behavioral and emotional symptoms.

- **Assignments:** Instruct the patient to continue with the Seizure Log and journal, relaxation method, tension reduction plan, self-observation, and/or goal setting, complete any Thought Records, and read Session 12, "Taking Control: An Ongoing Process."

- **Tools:** Help the patient to identify "other symptoms associated with seizures" and to facilitate a discussion.

Therapist Behaviors

The primary goal of Session 11 is to assist the patient in identifying sequelae associated with his or her seizures in order to normalize the inner experience, which can sometimes be disturbing and difficult to understand. The inner states or outer behaviors can lead a patient with seizures to feel more alone, out of control, and cut off from others due to a perception that no one else is able to understand.

Session 11 will help the patient become familiar with the different states of consciousness and types of behavior that make up "other symptoms." This information will enable patients to become more comfortable with themselves and more at home with the condition of seizures.

The content of this session is split into two major categories of "other symptoms": (1) inner states or sensations, and (2) types of behavior. Although many people may experience some of these symptoms, they are more common in people with seizures.

What Are the Common Altered States Experienced More Often by People With Seizures?

(The *Workbook* contains full descriptions of this list. Review the items that the patient experiences.)

- Déjà vu
- Jamais vu
- Dissociation
- Nonlinear thinking
- Scattered thinking
- Memory problems
- Out-of-body experiences
- Vertigo
- Crawling sensations
- Unpleasant stinging or jabbing sensations
- Premonitions
- Telepathy
- Religious and mystical experiences

What if the Patient Has "Other Symptoms" That Don't Correspond to Any Descriptions in This Chapter?

Encourage your patients to discuss other symptoms not described in the chapter. As noted above, unusual feelings and sensations occur more frequently in people with seizures. Session 11 gives patients the opportunity to have their experiences heard and validated. Encourage patients to create a list of personal altered states, sensations, or experiences that do not fit descriptions in the text.

What Is the Significance of These Various Altered States Described by the Patient?

Simply acknowledging to oneself and others that altered states are normal and expected for people with seizures can have a major impact in relieving anxiety about this subject. Let the patient know that science is just commencing research to understand these states.

Common Behavioral and Emotional Symptoms Experienced by People With Seizures

There are a wide variety of behavioral and emotional changes that may be experienced by individuals with seizures. In contrast to altered states that are apparent only to the individual who experiences them, some behavioral changes are more obvious to others than to the individual who is having them. For example, behavioral and emotional symptoms can be dramatically overt, such as anger expressed in fighting or yelling. On the other hand, the patient might have emotional changes that are both personal and subtle, such as mild mood swings, or feelings of anxiety or hurt.

Some behavioral and emotional symptoms represent the ways that individuals have learned to cope with their lives and their seizures, while others are a direct result of anticonvulsant medications or seizures themselves. The benefit of understanding their own behavioral and emotional changes is that patients can learn to observe and understand these changes, to minimize any negative impact on themselves and others, and to feel more comfortable with these "other symptoms" of seizures.

(The *Workbook* contains full descriptions of this list. Review the symptoms that the patient identified.)

- Depression
- A slowing of activity
- Increase in activity
- Anxiety
- Sudden outbursts of rage

Sometimes a Patient Behaves in Unusual Ways That Are Not Described in This Text. Is This Behavior One of the Patient's "Other Symptoms" of Seizures?

In all likelihood, the answer is "yes." As with the altered states and perceptual changes described above, some people with seizures experience unusual behavioral symptoms that are not described in the *Workbook*. The patient is encouraged to write down any unusual behaviors of "other symptoms" of seizures in his or her *Workbook* and to discuss this with you.

Review the concept that people with seizures have symptoms that other people might find unusual.

Read the session goal from the Workbook *aloud with the patient.*

Goal

The goal of this session is to recognize, accept, and cope positively with the inner states and sensations, and/or behavioral and emotional symptoms, that constitute "other symptoms" of seizures.

Obstacle

The patient is asked to identify potential obstacles to recognizing, accepting, and coping positively with inner states and sensations, and/or behavioral and emotional symptoms from a list of potential obstacles. Review the selected obstacles (e.g., difficulty noticing one's own unusual sensations or behavior; reluctance to reveal or discuss "weird" experiences—because of fear that others will judge these as crazy or unacceptable; feeling totally alone with these inner experiences—the sense that no one could possibly understand).

(For the full list of potential obstacles, refer to the Patient Workbook.*)*

Review Patient's In-Office Discussion Work

Review the patient's answers to the questions asked in the patient Workbook.

Obstacle

Can your patient identify other symptoms of seizures? Discuss how he or she feels about coping with other symptoms associated with seizures.

Tool

Review the "other symptoms" (listed above) with the patient and discuss any patient questions/concerns.

Relaxation Training

Review the patient's chosen relaxation method.

Closure Discussion

Use the structure of the Outcomes Response Grid (Table 15.1) during the time discussing patient impressions of what they learned and for feedback on progress.

Review of Completed Assignments

When reviewing the patient's in-office discussion work, review the patient's completed homework assignments.

1. Seizure Log / Thought Records
2. Tension Reduction Plan
3. Relaxation method
4. Journal keeping
5. At end of appointment, assign the final reading.

> ✓ Clinician Note
>
> *Session 11 marks the end of the formal treatment for NES using the* Workbook. *After having reviewed Session 11, the content of the final reading is briefly reviewed (as described in the next chapter) with the patient and assigned as a "parting gift." The primary message of the final reading is to emphasize that the end of treatment is only the beginning of "taking control" of one's seizures. With your help, the patient has been provided with numerous assignments and tools from the past sessions.*

The expectation is that the patient will utilize relevant session material in an ongoing, consistent manner for the rest of the patient's life.

Some patients describe anxiety about their final appointment. If needed and indicated, an appointment can be scheduled to discuss the final reading as the termination session. The next chapter in the Therapist Guide *covers the final reading material content and gives a structure if another appointment is scheduled as the termination session.*

Challenging or Problematic Responses

The seizure counselor introduced the session to the patient.

> P: "I have a lot of these symptoms discussed in this session. Like scattered thinking, premonitions and spiritual communications."

When a patient brings up spiritual content, ask how that applies in the everyday context. Your level of comfort with spiritual content will allow or suppress a patient's openness to discuss relevant issues. Spiritual experiences are not a *de facto* reflection of psychopathology or aberrant neurophysiology. Some "mystical" experiences are within the pale of orthodoxy in their respective practice. Some patients may have paranormal experiences that may or may not be ictally or psychiatrically related. Independent of the mechanism, sharing those experiences can be helpful for patients. Many patients will never have shared their numinous experiences before because of fear of being perceived as "crazy" or fear of potential stigmatization. The use of the biopsychosocialspiritual model and content in this session and prior sessions gives the patient the freedom to open up about significant experiences he or she may have experienced and did not have a place to discuss openly and freely with other clinicians. Focusing on the patient, this discussion can occur independent of the therapist's worldview.

CHAPTER 14

Taking Control: An Ongoing Process

(Corresponds to *Workbook* Chapter 13)

MATERIALS NEEDED/TASKS

- Seizure Log
- Journal
- Thought Record (TRs continue throughout; patient should have extra copies of the blank template)
- Tension Reduction Plan
- Relaxation method
- Self-observation and goal-setting
- Final reading: "Taking Control: An Ongoing Process"

APPOINTMENT OUTLINE

- Review homework assigned in the previous session.
- Briefly discuss the final reading, "Taking Control: An Ongoing Process."
- Termination: Discuss patient's impressions of how they have changed, and what they have learned during the treatment.

OVERVIEW

- **Goal:** The goal of the final reading is to help the patient find the balance of self-acceptance and self-responsibility as a future ongoing process.
- **Obstacle:** Self-blame and a lack of responsibility are discussed as potential obstacles to finding the balance of self-acceptance and self-responsibility as an ongoing process.

- **Assignments:** Encourage your patient to refer back to all provided assignments and tools in the patient *Workbook* as needed (e.g., setting goals, Thought Records, relaxation techniques, and journal writing).
- **Tools:** Review the three core areas discussed throughout the *Workbook*, including emotional insight, information about seizures, and a focus on a contented and healthy lifestyle for future guidance.

Therapist Behaviors

As noted in the previous chapter, Session 11 marks the end of formal treatment for nonepileptic seizures. After you review Session 11 with your patient, briefly review the content of the final reading and give this to the patient as a "parting gift." The primary message of the reading content is to emphasize that the end of treatment is only the beginning of "taking control" of one's seizures. With your help, the patient has been provided with numerous assignments and tools over the past 11 sessions. The expectation is that the patient will utilize relevant session material in an ongoing, consistent manner for the rest of his or her life.

The material in the final reading includes a brief discussion of the balance between self-acceptance and self-responsibility and the potential skewed self-perceptions when these two are out of balance. Showing the drawings in the appointment may reveal some experiences familiar to the patient. You and your patient may discuss how he or she may maintain a healthy balance and what to do if feeling out of balance.

Self-Acceptance and Self-Responsibility

Self-acceptance not only refers to accepting the pain, weakness, and lack of control that can accompany seizures, but it also means taking responsibility for one's seizures, taking control of living one's life to the fullest, and ultimately finding joy, contentment, and meaning.

Although all people have vulnerabilities that can be judged as weaknesses, individuals with seizures are at a particular disadvantage because they are unable to hide their seizures from others. As a result, other people may view one's seizures as a weakness and either respond negatively by not accepting the individual or by trying to protect the individual by treating him or her like an invalid.

Considering that other people are so often judgmental and express discomfort about seizures, it is not surprising that many people with seizures come to judge themselves as inadequate. By blaming themselves, patients are not taking responsibility for accepting themselves. On the other hand, if patients blame others for their seizures, or their lack of happiness or success, they are also avoiding responsibility for accepting themselves by becoming victims. Much of the *Workbook* has been concerned with these basic human dilemmas, to help people come to terms with what it means to take control of their seizures and their lives.

Common Pitfalls for People With Seizures

Drowning in Responsibility

The person who is drowning in responsibility has a lack of self-acceptance and a tendency to take too much responsibility for his or her own problems. This person might feel something like this: "I have to prove myself because I have seizures—I have to try to do more than anyone else. It's okay if my boss doesn't give me regular breaks, or any vacation; after all, he's given me a job even though I have seizures. If I can't make it under these conditions, it's my own fault."

Stuck in the Muck

On the other side of the spectrum, the victim who is stuck in the muck lacks an understanding that he or she has any power or responsibility to take care of personal difficulties. This victim is over-accepting of his or her own weaknesses and tends to blame others or hold others responsible for problems. Sometimes seen in people with a history of abuse, a person who is stuck in the muck might see the situation something like this: "I don't work—after all, I have seizures. My wife has to work to support both of us, and she does the housework and shopping, of course not very efficiently. She keeps busy and seems irritable most of the time, which makes my life miserable. I can't do anything about it because I have seizures."

Self-Acceptance and Self-Responsibility in Balance

The third alternative is to try to strike a balance between self-acceptance and self-responsibility. This dynamic balance involves liking and accepting yourself and at the same time taking responsibility for making your own life as fulfilling as it can be. A person who balances these two elements might view his or her situation something like this: "Having seizures certainly isn't easy, but I can learn to accept this hassle in my life and get on with things. I can still have a good job and earn the respect of my boss and colleagues. I can have a good relationship with my husband and do my part to work things out when problems come up. When setbacks arise, it's up to me to get through them and make my life what I want it to be."

Taking Control: An Ongoing Process

As noted above, the end of therapy is just the beginning of "taking control" of nonepileptic seizures. Over the course of the formal treatment appointments, the patient has been provided with numerous tools designed to help develop emotional insight, learn factual information about seizures, and foster lifestyle change.

During the course of treatment, the patient has confronted fear, anger, self-hate, and self-pity in order to reach self-acceptance. By removing the barriers to self-acceptance, the patient will be able to live life to the fullest. The factual information about nonepileptic seizures enables the patient to make decisions about medications as well as how to live harmoniously with seizures. Finally, the importance of making the decision to "take control," goal-setting, obtaining support, improving relationships, dealing with stresses, learning to relax, and enhancing personal wellness have given the patient the tools necessary to make his or her lifestyle compatible with his or her needs, whether physical, emotional, or spiritual.

CHAPTER 15 Prognosis (Patient Outcomes)

Patients Who Are Able to Take Control of Their Seizures

Taking control of one's seizures requires diligence and consistency with applying the tools learned in the *Workbook*. Although there is no way to predict outcome with any patient population, several patient characteristics appear to predict better results. In our experience, the successful patient embraces the nonepileptic seizure diagnosis and is motivated to feel better. Motivation is demonstrated through session attendance and completion of homework assignments. The successful patient understands that there will always be new problems and challenges that will have to be addressed. However, consistent application of the tools introduced in the *Workbook* and practice in treatment equip the patient to take on future stresses.

The process of "taking control" is a lifelong process. Although there will be setbacks along the way, the successful patient (1) rereads the *Workbook*; (2) uses healthy assertive communication; (3) sets new goals; (4) makes the links between triggers, negative states, and target symptoms; (5) completes Thought Records before, during, or after events; (6) reflects on internal and external stressors; (7) practices relaxation; and (8) has healthy boundaries in relationships. When setbacks do occur, the successful patient sits down with his or her journal and figures out what needs to be done to get back on track. Self-blame is to be avoided, and the importance of self-acceptance is emphasized. Everyone needs the help of others from time to time, and the successful patient seeks support in a healthy way from friends, family, faith, support groups, doctors, and seizure counselor.

Patients Who are Less Likely to Take Control of their Seizures

Specific characteristics have not been formally assessed allowing clinicians to directly link traits to poor outcome. Traits have not yet been studied prospectively in a comprehensive manner, as related to prognosis. Certain characteristics, however, have been observed in clinical care and in patients receiving treatment in some trials. Potential risks for the unsuccessful patient include (1) cluster B character pathology; (2) secondary gain (e.g., pending litigation, disability); (3) rejecting the diagnosis* (e.g., "the doctors and the monitoring have all missed what the events really are"); (4) repeatedly not doing homework; (5) missing sessions; (6) drug use (including minimizing marijuana used for pain, sleep, anxiety, etc.); (7) apathy (including, "nothing will help; I've given up"); (8) family overprotection or constant conflict; and (9) not letting go of the past.

Examples of Interactions Illustrating Healthy and Unhealthy Responses

Healthy Reflection

- SC: "How do you contain your seizures?"
- P: "I just converted my thoughts. When you have that warning, you think everyone is looking at you and waiting for you to have a seizure. They're really not, but you feel that way. So then I have to tell myself, 'Alter your thoughts and think of something else, think of something positive.' I've learned that from this program; before I would have just had a seizure."
- SC: "That's good that you've learned to use that technique."

The above is a good example of a patient using the session to reflect on his precursors and precipitants.

---

*It should be noted that anecdotal evidence suggests that nonacceptance of the nonepileptic seizure diagnosis does *not* mean that a patient will not benefit from treatment. For example, patients in this category have conveyed that just learning how to relax and learning how to sleep better improved their symptoms and lives.

Unhealthy Responses

> P: "I feel like, saying that 'I have NES' is basically saying, 'Well, we don't know what you have.' It's basically a catch-all term. Like, it's anything that is not epilepsy. This is about me working on myself, like the doctors have given up on me; like, damage control. Sure, I have negative emotions, and I have problems in my past, and sure this surfaced in a turbulent time, but I just don't think it is related to what is happening now. I can't expect you to help me at all. I guess I have to go this all alone."

In patients with cluster B personality, with a histrionic-borderline-narcissistic component, consider setting a limit and validating by normalizing the experience, with "You are very similar to many others with NES. What you've said is very commonly felt and stated among people with your history and symptoms."

Evaluating Outcomes

By the final session, a few different outcomes may occur regarding seizures, symptoms, and social functioning. Use the following framework to gauge progress.

Response Rate: Evaluating How They Did

Depending on the focus, patients may say they did great and are very pleased with the program, or they may say they did not receive any benefit. Seizures are not the only focus.

- **Seizures** may be fully responsive, partially responsive, or non-responsive to the intervention. Seizures are not the only outcome.
- **Comorbidities** may include depression, anxiety, PTSD, personality, pain, sleep, or other somatoform symptoms, among others. Some patients have improvement in their comorbidities along with their seizures, while others may have improvement in comorbidities even without seizure cessation.
- **Functioning** is another area of focus. Seizures may continue, but the patient is now able to go out again with an improved quality of life.

Patients who have full response in all three areas may not need further follow-up. Patients with partial or no response in some of the areas may require maintenance therapy or booster sessions. Patients who have familial conflicts may benefit from a few sessions with the nuclear and family of origin members present to address the transactional patterns of the family. This can be discussed in the closing appointment.

Completing the following grid with the patient in the termination appointment may give some perspective on what was accomplished and what work is left to be done. If a patient elects to continue in treatment, therapeutic targets can be identified from prior "stuck-points" for the paitient, to give direction to future appointments, (e.g. more work on healthy assertive communication, relationships with family members, identifying and processing Hot Thoughts/Core Beliefs on Thought Records, working through past traumatic experiences, etc.).

Table 15.1 Outcomes Response Grid

	Seizures	Symptom Comorbidities	Social Functioning
Full response			
Partial response			
No response			

✓ Therapy Notes: Dealing With Disappointment

By the end of treatment, there is a hope that patients will have complete resolution of their seizures and will have returned to pre-symptom functioning. In the cases when that does not happen, people are disappointed, including the patient, the family, and the provider. The patient and family came to you and just wanted "the old person back before the seizures started." The clinician wanted to be "the good doctor" who made the patient well. When those outcomes are not achieved, acknowledge the disappointment of persisting symptoms and then reframe. Discuss areas of improvement or growth, despite the lack of desired response.

CHAPTER 16

When the Patient has a Seizure in the Office Setting

Given the nature of nonepileptic seizures, it is not uncommon for patients to have seizures in session and in the waiting room. This can be disquieting for staff members, family, and other patients. In order to ensure a unified approach toward addressing a patient's seizures, staff members should be educated about the nature and presentation of the illness. Although the natural reaction is to go into "emergency mode," staff members should be instructed to briefly ensure that the patient is safe (e.g., not bumping head against a wall) and to otherwise leave the patient alone. As noted previously, the tendency to rush to aid, call 911, and "hover" around a patient experiencing a nonepileptic seizure is contraindicated for treating the patient because this behavior reinforces potential secondary gain the patient achieves from the seizure (e.g., attention) or it "feeds" the patient's illness identity (e.g., the patient becomes the illness).

One patient observed,

"In the beginning it made me more nervous when people went into the 'emergency mode' when I had a seizure. It made me feel like, 'Oh my God I need help!' Now that I know what it is and I know that it is not going to hurt me, I get angry when someone starts to hover over me. I am not helpless, I know what is going to happen; I just ride it out and just push through it. I can come out of it quicker if you just leave me alone."

"One day I had a seizure in a restaurant. My brother and sister carried me out to the parking lot. My brother touched me to comfort me and it made it so much worse. My sister did the same thing and it made it worse. People's natural reaction is to comfort you, but if you do that it just makes it worse. I know that I just need to be left alone and work through it."

The same patient relayed negative experiences she had with professionals who did not feel comfortable when she experienced a seizure. She noted,

"If you're not comfortable with seizures, then you're freaking the patient out."

Similarly, family members should be discouraged from rushing to help the patient. They should be informed that the nonepileptic seizure treatment is about learning how to "take control" of one's seizures, rather than being controlled by them. In our experience, some family members struggle with this approach and even become angry with the seizure counselor (e.g., "But she's our daughter, how can we *not* help her?"). Family members should be reassured that the patient can benefit from the strategies learned in treatment.

Finally, other patients might become alarmed or even upset when witnessing a patient having a nonepileptic seizure. Witnesses should be reassured that the patient is okay and safe, and this can be demonstrated by speaking in a calm, authoritative voice.

When the Patient Has a Seizure During a Session

As noted above, it is common for a patient to have a seizure during an appointment. When this occurs, the seizure counselor should ensure that the patient is out of harm's way and then leave the patient alone. Once the seizure ends, the event should be used as an opportunity to reinforce session material (e.g., identifying triggers or auras). As the seizure counselor, avoid taking a reactionary approach to a patient's seizure given that this would be antithetical to the treatment program (i.e., taking control of one's seizures).

A seizure in the appointment can indicate that the patient may have been pushed to an emotional limit or exhausted cognitive/emotional resources. Allowing the patient to move into difficult areas when ready (e.g., where the patient generates the content of the Thought Record) can (1) help the patient address challenging areas, and (2) modulate emotions/thoughts at a level/pace comfortable to the patient.

The goal in this modality is to take the person to the edge but not push him or her over the cliff. The nuanced nature of the therapy is seen when you move through a difficult place and your patient maintains control. You will be present with the patient as he or she looks into the abyss, and you will walk together with the patient through the dark places. As noted in the Introduction, this is the essence of "abiding," bearing with your patients, as they explore their humanity, their pain, and their recovery.

Abiding involves both content and process, where you walk into and through very difficult places with the patient. With abiding, you do not force the patient into a place where she or he is not ready to go, psychologically or emotionally. Rather, the patient approaches the problem area(s)—including past or present trauma, abuse, or neglect—once he or she has made the link among triggers, negative states, and target symptoms, and is equipped with tools to address external stressors and internal issues. In abiding with the patient, he or she has the structure and trust to look into the chaos of past events, painful experiences, and how those may relate to present circumstances. "Abiding" means that you will not abandon your patient when times are tough, for the patient (or for you).

The Power of Words

In this intervention, you have seen the impact and importance of words. In our patients with histories of trauma and abuse, words in the past were used to tear down. In this therapy, words are used to rebuild. With compassion, empathy, honest reflection, reason and words of truth (embodied as, *logos,* in Greek), the seizure counselor can help the patient to establish a narrative that provides wholeness and healing. Rather than using neurostimulation with electrodes (e.g., Vagal Nerve Stimulation, Deep Brain Stimulation, Transcranial Magnetic Stimulation) for activating synapses and channels, in this treatment, seizure reduction and improvement in comorbid depression and anxiety can come from "logo-modulation" using words that targets emotions, cognitions and behaviors.

Although it is natural for any of us to express concern for those in distress, you must refrain from engaging in behavior that reinforces the positive attention a patient receives for having a seizure.

- SC: "OK, can you use relaxation to stop the seizure? Ok, let me know when you come back to yourself (seizure stopped)."
- P: (still post-ictal and unresponsive)
- SC: "OK, you feel better now?"

Displaying compassion is important, but relevant to the therapy process and to help the patient learn to take control, the question during or after the seizure is not, "Do you feel better now?" Rather, ask, "So, what do you think just happened?" and let the patient evaluate and interpret. This places the responsibility of processing the event on the patient. Also, during the seizure, one way you can check on the patient (and show that you are present and aware and not merely ignoring the behavior) is to say, "Let me know when you are back with us." You can give a cognitive task to the patient once the patient has returned to baseline, such as, "I want you to remember the words 'blue elephant.'" After the seizure, ask the patient if those words can be recalled. If aware, or unaware, discuss the similarities/differences of this seizure to the patient's other seizures and how that awareness can be used for any possible future seizures.

When working with a patient who has nonepileptic seizures, it is likely that the patient will have a seizure in your presence and in the presence of others at some point. How you react to a patient having a seizure can be beneficial or detrimental. Taking control of one's seizures is the central theme of this treatment. Although it is human nature to want to aid someone in distress, overreacting to a patient having a seizure reinforces the "sick role" identity, which keeps the patient mired in the illness, or it can reinforce secondary gain that some patients consciously or subconsciously receive from the illness. As long as the patient is not harming him- or herself during a seizure, the optimal reaction is to acknowledge that the patient is having a seizure in a calm manner and to inform the patient that treatment will resume once the seizure ends.

CHAPTER 17 ⟩ Workbook Appendices

Appendix I: Biofeedback

Some individuals and counselors may choose to use biofeedback training to augment relaxation training. Biofeedback procedures detailed in Appendix I are guidelines that the Andrews/Reiter Epilepsy Research Program has utilized with biofeedback training.

Specific Instructions That Facilitate Biofeedback Training

The goal of relaxation training sessions utilizing biofeedback equipment for persons with seizures is to teach them to reach and sustain an awake, relaxed state.

The biofeedback therapist should observe for regional muscle tension during the exercise, particularly in the early training sessions. It will be necessary to work with patients to help them relax these muscles. Sometimes verbal suggestions to "open the jaw," "relax the chin," and "let go of any tension in the forehead" will suffice.

It is helpful to explain that seizures may occur in a drowsy state, which is the reason for learning to avoid it with relaxation training. If your patient is unable to reach a fully relaxed state, encourage the patient by telling him or her to "let go" even more, with positive suggestions that "you can do it." If your patient appears sleepy, provide a problem to solve to wake him or her up. You may also utilize autogenic techniques, visualization or positive thoughts (if those were helpful in biofeedback sessions 2 and 3).

Tell your patient that the goal is to keep in the awake, relaxed state as much as possible during the session.

Protocol for EEG Biofeedback Training Sessions

The protocol for instructing your patient during biofeedback training is established in the first biofeedback training session found in Appendix I of the *Workbook*. Biofeedback training sessions 2–6 build on this to include more advanced levels of auditory feedback signals and introduce key techniques, including progressive muscle relaxation, deep breathing, and visualization and/or positive thoughts exercises.

Basic settings to be used with the biofeedback equipment are outlined in the first biofeedback training appointment. With each subsequent appointment, the biofeedback machine window settings are gradually increased to achieve auditory feedback at 8–12 cps, greater than 50 μv. The settings depend on what the patient has accomplished, never pushing the setting amplitude to a greater level than he or she is ready for. Follow the specific instructions detailed in each biofeedback training session in Appendix I.

Once patients have reached the goal of being able to go into an awake relaxed state at 8–12 cps, 50–150 μv, they will spend time in sessions learning how to use this new skill. Tell the patient to change brain wave states when tense or over-aroused, when experiencing a powerful emotion such as anger or fear, and when aware of the pre-seizure aura. Between training sessions, patients should work on taking a deep diaphragmatic breath and trying to change brain wave state to awake, relaxed whenever feeling the need to do so.

Appendix II: Yoga

What Is "Yoga"?

When thinking of yoga, most people in the West imagine an incredibly fit and flexible body that bends into positions that far exceed the range of motion of an average person's joints. But those visual images of yoga reflect the Western perspective of yoga, which is often dominated by an external, somewhat superficial measurement of success.

Yoga is not about what a posture looks like from the outside. It is about what it looks like from the inside of the person doing it. It is about finding and accepting the balance between the follow-through of yoga instructions and personal assessment of what seems to be right in the moment. Therein lies one of yoga's most powerful tools: The recognition of the validity of inner guidance and that sustainable happiness can only be found if the student deliberately detaches from the motivation to succeed.

The term "yoga" summarizes many different traditions. Each tradition encompasses techniques that are geared toward integration of the human mind, body, and personality. Depending on the tradition, one will find commonly practiced physical postures intermixed with breathing exercises, contemplative practices, ethical guidelines, and philosophic ideas.

How Does the Patient Decide if Yoga Is Appropriate?

The key to understanding the potential benefits of yoga is to establish a regular practice. Yoga is an action, present, habit-oriented discipline. Yoga teachers emphasize that good yoga practice combines regular attendance at classes with regular practice at home. Joining a yoga class not only allows one to practice yoga under the guidance of an experienced teacher, it also has a social component. It allows one to spend time in the company of other participants. One of the rewarding features of practicing yoga in a group is a feeling of community that occurs with little verbal communication between participants.

✓ **Clinician Note**

If the patient has an EEG that shows epileptiform changes during hyperventilation, avoid techniques that include fast and heavy breathing.

Resources for Further Reading are listed at the end of the *Workbook* Appendix II.

You can use the following guidelines to introduce your patient to meditation:

First: Select a focus for concentration during your meditation sessions. Consider using a phrase, prayer, mantra, or scripture verse; you may want to select one that has particular meaning for you, such as, "Lord Have Mercy." Or you might select a visual image, such as a candle flame, a cross, a Buddha, or a different spiritual picture. Some people use breathing as a focus.

Second: Set aside 10–20 minutes of uninterrupted time daily for meditation practice. Sit comfortably in a straight-backed chair or cross-legged on the floor. As with relaxation exercises, meditation begins with allowing your body to relax. Adjust your position and clothing until you feel comfortable; then try to keep your body still throughout the meditation session. Let your breathing become slow and relaxed. Scan your entire body for tension, releasing tension and relaxing deeply as you do so. You may want to do a brief version of the relaxation exercise described in Session 6.

Third: Now that your body feels more relaxed, sit quietly while you think of the words or image you have selected as the focus for your meditation. Concentrate on this focus, allowing other thoughts and feelings to pass without judgment or comment. Cultivate an uncritical, quiet, compassionate attitude toward yourself and your meditation efforts. Whenever you notice other thoughts, simply let them go, refocusing your attention on the object of your meditation.

✓ A Word of Caution Regarding Meditation

Some individuals with seizures may experience increased seizure activity during initial attempts to meditate simply because the mind tends to become more active when the body is still, with decreased sensory input. Suppressed feelings that may surface during meditation can be valuable for the process of taking control but also may activate the patient temporarily. We therefore recommend that individuals who want to establish a meditation practice for relaxation purposes either use scriptural meditation, guided meditation (e.g., mindfulness meditation by

---

> *Jon Kabat-Zinn, Judeo-Christian meditation by Richard Foster or similar programs) or seek the guidance of an experienced teacher. If you have experience with meditation, you may choose to guide your patient yourself, or you may refer your patient to a respected meditation teacher.*

Resources for Further Reading are listed at the end of *Workbook* Appendix III.

References

Beck, A. T. *Cognitive Therapy of Personality Disorders*. New York: Guilford Press, 1990.

Beck, J. S. *Cognitive Therapy: Basics and Beyond*. New York: Guilford Press, 1995.

Ehrmann, Joe. *Inside Out Coaching*. New York: Simon & Schuster, 2011.

Greenberger, D., & Padesky, C. A. *Mind Over Mood*. New York: Guilford Press, 1995.

LaFrance, W. C., Jr., & Devinsky, O. Treatment of nonepileptic seizures. *Epilepsy & Behavior*, 2002;3:S19–23.

LaFrance, W. C., Jr., & Friedman, J. H. Cognitive behavioral therapy for psychogenic movement disorder. *Movement Disorders*, 2009;24:1856–1857.

LaFrance, W. C., Jr., Miller I. W., Ryan, C. E., Blum, A. S., Solomon, D. A., Kelley, J. E., & Keitner, G. I. Cognitive behavioral therapy for psychogenic nonepileptic seizures. *Epilepsy & Behavior*, 2009;14:591–596.

LaFrance, W. C., Jr., Baird, G. L., Barry, J. J., Blum, A. S., Frank Webb, A., Keitner, G. I., Machan, J. T., Miller, I., & Szaflarski, J. P. Multicenter pilot treatment trial for psychogenic nonepileptic seizures: a randomized clinical trial. *JAMA Psychiatry*, 2014;71:997–1005.

LaFrance, W. C., Jr., Baker, G. A., Duncan, R., Goldstein, L. H., & Reuber, M. Minimum requirements for the diagnosis of psychogenic nonepileptic seizures: a staged approach: a report from the International League Against Epilepsy Nonepileptic Seizures Task Force. *Epilepsia*, 2013;54:2005–2018.

Padesky, C. A. Schema change processes in cognitive therapy. *Clinical Psychology & Psychotherapy*, 1994;1(5):267–278.

Reiter, J., Andrews, D., & Janis, C. *Taking Control of Your Epilepsy*. A Workbook for Patients and Professionals. 1st ed. Santa Rosa, CA: The Basics; 1987.

Schachter, S. C., & LaFrance, W. C., Jr., eds. *Gates and Rowan's Nonepileptic Seizures*, 3rd ed. Cambridge; New York: Cambridge University Press, 2010.

W. Curt LaFrance, Jr., MD, MPH, is Director of Neuropsychiatry and Behavioral Neurology at Rhode Island Hospital (RIH) and Assistant Professor of Psychiatry and Neurology at Alpert Medical School, Brown University. He is the neuropsychiatrist for the RIH Comprehensive Epilepsy Program and a faculty member of the Brown Institute for Brain Science. He studied at Wake Forest University (BA in psychology), Medical College of Georgia (MD) and Brown University (MPH). He trained in Brown's combined residency in Neurology and Psychiatry and is double boarded. His research is in neuropsychiatric aspects of epilepsy, somatoform / conversion disorders, and traumatic brain injury. He is co-editor of *Gates and Rowan's Nonepileptic Seizures.*

Jeffrey Peter Wincze, PhD, received his PhD in clinical psychology from Boston University, and he worked and completed post-doctoral training at the Center for Anxiety and Related Disorders at Boston University. He has been involved in federally funded research grants investigating the assessment and treatment of anxiety disorders. He is currently a Staff Psychologist at Rhode Island Hospital and he is a Clinical Assistant Professor of Psychiatry and Human Behavior at Brown University. He has published articles in the areas of anxiety disorders, compulsive hoarding, and biofeedback. His current research is focused on management of depression and treatment of conversion disorders.

Printed in the USA/Agawam, MA
July 27, 2018